"*Lydia: Paul's Cosmopolitan Hostess* is a ł comprehensive, and absorbing introdu within the community supporting Paul provides substantial access to the most recent research into the social web of relations that characterized the Pauline network, focusing in particular on the roles women could and did play, and the shape of the domestic and public spaces they inhabited. Ascough does an excellent job of presenting multiple sources and background information, thus allowing readers to come to their own conclusions. This book is a marvelous addition to the study of Paul and will be an essential resource in a variety of contexts where people are studying Paul and the world he inhabited."

> —*Mary E. Hess*
> Associate Professor of Educational Leadership
> Luther Seminary
> St. Paul, MN

"Richard Ascough's *Lydia* is a marvelous work of erudition and clarity, which uses the little-known figure of Lydia to elaborate important aspects of the social world of the earliest Jesus movement. We learn about mobility, life in a Roman colony, Mediterranean family structures, slavery, the nature of marriage, civic values, private patronage, household piety, and the public and private roles of women. Ascough deftly sketches the Mediterranean world of ancient Christianity through the eyes of one woman of Philippi."

> —*John S. Kloppenborg*
> Professor and Chair
> Department & Centre for the Study of Religion
> University of Toronto

"Richard Ascough's in-depth knowledge of history and Scripture guide his disciplined imagination to create a thick description of the woman named Lydia. Her two cameo appearances in the Acts of the Apostles leave contemporary readers yearning for more. Readers of *Lydia: Paul's Cosmopolitan Hostess* will come away with a focused and detailed rendering of first-century lifeways in Philippi, the place of women within the world of the Roman Empire, and an appreciation of how the message of Jesus took hold and grew. Lydia, thanks to Ascough's careful research and reading, emerges as a deeply spiritual and worldly wise figure relevant to 21st-century women and men. This book will intrigue all sensitive and curious readers of the New Testament."

—*Dr. Peter Gilmour*
Professor Emeritus
Loyola University
Institute of Pastoral Studies

Paul's Social Network: Brothers and Sisters in Faith

Bruce J. Malina, Series Editor

Lydia

Paul's Cosmopolitan Hostess

Richard S. Ascough

A Michael Glazier Book

LITURGICAL PRESS

Collegeville, Minnesota

www.litpress.org

A Michael Glazier Book published by Liturgical Press

Cover design by Ann Blattner. *Saint Paul*, fresco fragment, Roma, 13th century.

1   2   3   4   5   6   7   8   9

Library of Congress Cataloging-in-Publication Data

Ascough, Richard S.
    Lydia : Paul's cosmopolitan hostess / Richard S. Ascough.
      p.   cm. — (Paul's social network, brothers and sisters in faith)
    "A Michael Glazier Book."
    Includes bibliographical references and indexes.
    ISBN 978-0-8146-5269-5 (pbk.)
    1. Bible. N.T. Acts XVI, 14-15, 40—Criticism, interpretation, etc.
2. Lydia (Biblical figure)   3. Women in the Bible.   4. Paul, the Apostle, Saint—Friends and associates.   I. Title.

  BS2625.52.A83 2008
  226.6'092—dc22   2008046744

In memory
Beatrice Ascough
(1942–2007)

CONTENTS

LIST OF FIGURES

PREFACE

Human beings are embedded in a set of social relations. A social network is one way of conceiving that set of social relations in terms of a number of persons connected to one another by varying degrees of relatedness. In the early Jesus group documents featuring Paul and coworkers, it takes little effort to envision the apostle's collection of friends and friends of friends that is the Pauline network.

This set of brief books consists of a description of some of the significant persons who constituted the Pauline network. For Christians of the Western tradition, these persons are significant ancestors in faith. While each of them is worth knowing by themselves, it is largely because of their standing within that web of social relations woven about and around Paul that they are of lasting interest. Through this series we hope to come to know those persons in ways befitting their first-century Mediterranean culture.

Bruce J. Malina
Creighton University
Series Editor

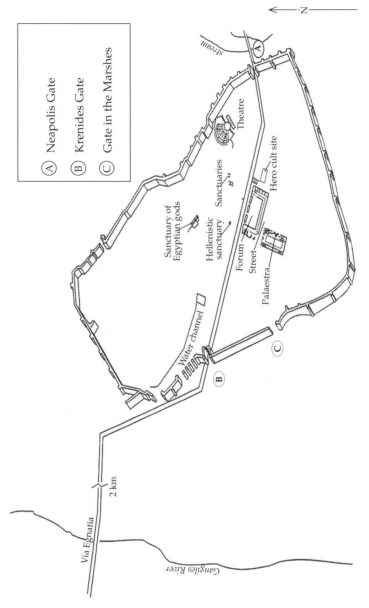

Figure 1. Plan of Philippi

INTRODUCTION

Who Is Lydia?

Not much is known about Lydia beyond what Luke narrates in three verses—Acts 16:14-15, 40. She appears nowhere else in the New Testament, not even a mention in the letter Paul sent to Philippi, the urban center in which Lydia was the first to come to believe in Jesus. Unlike the case of other women in the New Testament, women such as Mary Magdalene and Elizabeth, the later traditions about Lydia are few. Even the rather hefty third edition of *The Oxford Dictionary of the Christian Church* has no entry on "Lydia," which is indicative of the marginalization of the role she played. Yet Lydia was the host and patron of the first community of Jesus followers established in the land mass that would later be known as Europe, and she was the nexus for the network of Jesus believers in and around Philippi. Paul's letter to the Philippians suggests that even at its early stages this Jesus group was a vibrant and thriving community, one that filled Paul with joy (Phil 1:3-4; 4:1). Without Lydia there may well have been no Philippian Jesus community. She was a key player in Paul's social network—one of the pivotal sisters in the faith.

1

Luke's Narrative

Luke's account of the travels of the change agents responsible for the formation of early Jesus groups places Paul and Silas in the Roman province of Macedonia during Paul's second journey. Philippi became their gateway into Macedonia (the northern region of modern Greece), having already traveled through Galatia and Asia Minor (located in the central and western regions of modern-day Turkey). They had attempted to go north to the province of Bithynia, on the coast of the Black Sea, but were prevented by "the Spirit of Jesus" (Acts 16:7), who apparently had other plans. Having rerouted to the coastal city of Troas in the northwest of Asia Minor, Paul lay down for a restful night. It was not to be. Luke writes, "During the night Paul had a vision: there stood a man of Macedonia pleading with him and saying, 'Come over to Macedonia and help us'" (Acts 16:9). In the morning new plans were laid, and the traveling companions set sail across the top of the Aegean Sea.

At this point in Luke's narrative we find a grammatical oddity. The narrator's voice switches suddenly from the third person ("*they* did such-and-such") to the first person ("*we* did such-and-such"). This is the first of several passages narrated in the first person, which are known as the "we passages." Curiously, the first of these passages begins with the travelers leaving Troas and sailing for Philippi (Acts 16:11). It concludes just as suddenly following the story of Lydia and at the opening of a story about a demon-possessed slave girl (Acts 16:17). The next "we passage" occurs some chapters later but is again associated with Troas and Philippi: "They went ahead and were waiting for us in Troas; but we sailed from Philippi after the days of Unleavened Bread, and in five days we joined them in Troas, where we stayed for seven days" (Acts 20:5-6). From here the narrative remains in the first person for much, but not all, of the voyage by ship along the coast of Asia Minor and across the Mediterranean to Jerusalem (Acts 10:5-15; 21:1-18), switching back to third person until Paul is sent to Rome in chains and is again joined by our unnamed "we" narrator, who experiences with Paul the shipwreck on Malta (Acts 27:1–28:16).

We do not want to pause too long here for lessons in grammar or a full discussion of the peculiarities of the narrative styles of ancient literary genres. For our purposes, however, it is well worth noting that the first-person narration of the story of Lydia has raised the possibility for some scholars that an eyewitness was present to observe, and later record, the events. Some suggest it was the writer of Acts himself, which later tradition associates with the name "Luke." Certainly the writer of Acts has no problem injecting his own voice into his document since he does so in Acts 1:1 and in Luke 1:3. Others have suggested that the writer of Acts was not himself present but had access to some source material written by someone who was—a distinct possibility since Luke admits to the use of sources for his two-volume work (Luke 1:1-4; cf. Acts 1:1). Still others discount the eyewitness nature of the narratives, attributing the use of the first person to Luke's creative writing style.

I find myself drawn to the conclusion that Luke is using a first-person source in these passages. Although in modern writings we would expect the use of sources to be properly footnoted, this was not the case in antiquity, and Luke's switch of pronoun is sufficient to indicate that a source has been incorporated into the narrative. Nevertheless, like many other students of the New Testament, I do not think Luke has used this source without at least some heavy-handed editing. When we compare Luke's narrative of Jesus in the gospel to one of Luke's primary sources, the Gospel of Mark, we find a writer who is willing to follow his source for many of the details but to adjust, nuance, delete, and supplement them when it becomes necessary, usually in order to present more clearly Luke's own theological and social concerns. There is no reason to expect he has done any differently in writing Acts, although we do not, unfortunately, have any independent sources with which to compare it. Modern scholars are left with the task of sorting out what in Acts comes from the sources and traditions at Luke's disposal, what is from the hand of Luke (and thus is "redactional"), and what, if anything, is historical.[1] The framework of Acts is secondary and Luke has compressed into one account incidents that may have happened on separate visits to a city, yet many of the incidents themselves may reflect reliable data. It remains to be seen what if anything can be viewed as reliable data for Lydia, and this will occupy some of our attention in the following chapters. First, however, we must look briefly at the passage itself.

In Acts 16:11-15 Luke narrates the travel of Paul and his cohort to Philippi and their subsequent encounter with a group of women gathered at a riverside outside one of the gates of Philippi:

> We set sail from Troas and took a straight course to Samothrace, the following day to Neapolis, and from there to Philippi, which is a leading city of the district of Macedonia and a Roman colony. We remained in this city for some days. On the sabbath day we went outside the gate by the river, where we supposed there was a place of prayer; and we sat down and spoke to the women who had gathered there. A certain woman named Lydia, a worshiper of God, was listening to us; she was from the city of Thyatira and a dealer in purple cloth. The Lord opened her heart to listen eagerly to what was said by Paul. When she and her household were baptized, she urged us, saying, "If you have judged me to be faithful to the Lord, come and stay at my home." And she prevailed upon us.

There then intervenes a rather lengthy narrative in which Paul and Silas run afoul of a slave owner, who has them incarcerated. A well-timed earthquake, seemingly localized just at the jailer's house-jail, results in the two companions gaining their freedom. At this point, Luke returns ever so briefly to Lydia: "After leaving the prison they went to Lydia's home; and when they had seen and encouraged the brothers and sisters there, they departed" (Acts 16:40).

A number of elements of Lydia's background and social position can be gleaned from both the explicit and implicit information Luke provides in the narrative of Acts:

- Her name is Lydia.
- She is a businesswoman—a dealer in cloth dyed purple and/or purple dye itself.[2]
- She comes from the city of Thyatira (which is in Asia Minor).
- She owns a house in Philippi.
- She has oversight of a household.
- She has particular cultic commitments as a "worshiper of God."
- She gathers, perhaps regularly, with other women.
- Their gathering takes place at a "place of prayer" on a riverbank.

As Paul and his companions sit and talk with the women, Lydia comes to believe in Jesus and is baptized. Here we learn a little bit more about Lydia:

- She is receptive to the spiritual realm.
- She is hospitable.
- She opens her home as a meeting place for others.

The details given for Lydia are in stark contrast to Luke's description of Paul's work in the other major Macedonian cities of Thessalonica and Beroea (Acts 17:1-17), suggesting that for Philippi there is good reason to trust the veracity of the account. Nevertheless, Luke's proclivity for presenting men and women of substance as founding members of Jesus groups means this presentation of Lydia must be used with caution.

We can proceed based on the evidence in Acts by assuming that the foundation of the Philippian Jesus group might well have been a house-based group, the patron of which was an independent businesswoman named Lydia. Nevertheless, each aspect as presented in the above list is not without challenging interpretive problems and deserves close study, which will be our task in the remainder of this book. Two other issues bear initial comment, however. The first issue concerns Paul's role in the passage, since it is central to Luke's narrative, although of only passing interest to us in our study of Lydia. As is the case throughout Acts, Paul functions in the Lydia story as a change agent—a person who communicates a message about an innovative social movement or product and seeks to influence others toward adopting this innovation. Only some of the seven typical tasks of a change agent are present in the story, but others are implicit.[3] As a change agent Paul needs to influence the leadership of the riverside meeting toward accepting the need for change, which is likely why Lydia is singled out to become the first adopter. He also must establish a relationship of information exchange, which again Paul does up front, not by preaching, but by sitting down alongside the gathered women and speaking with them (Acts 16:13). As a change agent Paul must create cognitive dissonance between the present beliefs and practices of the women and their desire for a particular kind of engagement with the divine realm. This, in turn, creates a desire for change. In the Acts narrative, however, credit for this task is shared between Paul and God, who "opened her [Lydia's] heart to listen eagerly to what was said by Paul" (Acts 16:14). This eagerness is translated into action when Lydia chooses baptism for herself and her household as a symbolic ritual of change. Before change agents can move on to new areas they must ensure that the new behaviors of their clients have been firmly grounded, which is why Paul returns to Lydia's house to see and encourage the brothers and sisters there (Acts 16:40). Once assured, Paul departs east toward Thessalonica.

The second issue needing comment concerns Lydia's name. Some scholars suggest that the name "Lydia" may be an ethnic appellation that designates her place of origin, as Luke indicates she was originally from Thyatira, a city in the area called Lydia. If it is an ethnic appellation it would indicate that at one time

Lydia was a slave who had been freed. A number of inscriptions suggesting that several people involved in the purple trade were ex-slaves might imply that she was herself a freed slave. However, two first- or second-century inscriptions attest to women of status who used the name Lydia, making the assumption of former servile status somewhat conjectural. Her status as a free person, either freeborn or freed slave, is indicated by her control over a household and a house. At the same time, it is doubtful that Lydia was a Roman citizen, as she is associated with her work, rather than the name of her family.[4]

Civic Contexts

At the beginning of this introduction we noted some key issues in coming to know Lydia and the help that can be offered by a close examination of Acts using the tools that come from a method called historical criticism. This method has served scholars well for generations and has led, and continues to lead, to some interesting and stimulating results. Nevertheless, the range of questions it can answer and conclusions it can draw is limited, and new methods have been developed that broaden our understanding of New Testament documents. Different methods yield different results. As the human sciences have developed in disciplines such as anthropology, sociology, and psychology, New Testament scholars have come to recognize that the documents we read are more than simply words. They reflect specific social systems of real people in real social and historical contexts. Biblical documents are "multidimensional phenomena" and are open to a variety of methods of interpretation, including ones that attempt "to identify the social and cultural world portrayed in the text as well as try to identify the various actors' motives for action."[5]

Social-scientific approaches to New Testament documents were pioneered by the work of Bruce Malina, Jerome Neyrey, John Pilch, John Elliott, and other members of the Context Group, an

ongoing gathering of biblical scholars. Their methodological insights inform the dominant approach in our study of Lydia as we
employ historical-critical study and sociological-anthropological
methods and theories in what is increasingly becoming an interdisciplinary approach to the New Testament. Our study of Lydia
is an attempt to balance an understanding of the *typical* behaviors
of first-century circum-Mediterranean peoples through the use
of social science modeling with an analysis of the idiosyncrasies
and distinctive behaviors found in particular times and places
through literary and archaeological studies. Whether or not we
can determine the historicity of the details in the narrative about
Lydia, or even if there was a historical Lydia, these methods allow
us to gauge what Luke's readers would have assumed about
Lydia and, more important, they help us see Lydia as representative of a type of female believer active in the network of Paul's
coworkers in the early Jesus groups.

We want to begin with one of the fundamental assumptions
about persons in antiquity that we will have in mind throughout
our study of Lydia, namely, her own self-understanding. There
are a variety of ways in which people are aware of the self, rang-
ing from a sense of being unique and independent (individualism) to a sense of sharing most things in common with a
kinship group or subgroup (collectivism). Modern North
American society is dominated by individualism, in which the
personal goals of the individual are given priority, whereas the
first-century Mediterranean world was characterized by collectivism, in which the goals of the group were prioritized.
This difference affects how we understand the documents we
read and the actions of the characters therein. Mediterranean
persons

> were all group-oriented selves, very concerned to adopt
> the viewpoints of the groups (their in-groups) whose fate
> they shared. They would never have considered Jesus as a
> personal Lord and Savior or as a personal Redeemer. If
> anything, Jesus was the church's (the group's) Lord and

> Savior, and it was by belonging to the church (the group)
> that one experienced the presence of the Lord.[6]

In this type of context persons rely on others to form opinions about themselves, particularly the most important person in their social network, usually coming from within their immediate kin group. Such people are not individualists but "dyadics" or "doublists." They are outwardly, or publicly, oriented rather than internally oriented and give little attention or significance to individual consciousness and thought; they have an "anti-introspective self."[7]

As with individualism, collectivism is something that one is socialized into from birth—in such a culture it is rare to find anyone who can conceive of it differently, at least not without significant emotional and intellectual effort. The following chart describes differences between individualism and collectivism as they are generally conceived. It is framed in such a way that the reader can put checkmarks in all that apply to her or him personally. It is likely that those who are predominantly formed within Western contexts (e.g., North America, Western Europe) will find they have more checkmarks in the individualism column. Those formed in non-Western contexts (e.g., China, Africa, Middle East) will find they have more checkmarks in the collectivism column. Nevertheless, there may be times when the reader checks a box that is in the atypical column or, at the very least, when the reader puzzles for a while about which side to check. This reveals, in a small way, a core methodological issue with social-scientific modeling—the models deal with generalities not specifics. Due to the influence of travel, communication, and intercultural contact, modern persons are formed by multiple factors, which means any one of us may not fit completely into one side or the other. The same is true, albeit to a much lesser degree, for those living in the circum-Mediterranean in antiquity. Nevertheless, as a general guide, those of us living in the West today are most like individualists, while those living in the ancient Mediterranean world were most like collectivists.[8]

	Individualist	**Collectivist**
Primary Responsibility	Looks out for oneself first and perhaps one's immediate family. One's responsibility for others is quite loose.	Part of a strong cohesive ingroup from birth (extended family, village members, friends, etc.) to which one must remain unquestionably loyal, and from which one receives protection. Self-sacrifice and subordination of one's interests to those of the group are required.
Identity	Defines oneself in terms of personal attributes. Individual uniqueness and self-determination are valued. One promotes self-expression, individual thinking, and personal choice.	Defines oneself in terms of group attributes. Conformity to the group norms is valued. One promotes adherence to norms and respect for authority and/or elders and works toward group consensus.
Goals	Prioritizes one's personal goals. Self-satisfaction or "actualization" is primary.	Personal goals are subsumed into the goals of one's ingroups. Group flourishing is primary.
Social Encounters	More likely to prejudge people based on obvious personal attributes.	More likely to prejudge people based on group identity.
Social Interaction	Bluntly honest with others and will tackle tough issues head-on in order to get at the truth or the correct answer.	Avoids blunt honesty and sensitive issues, sometimes exhibiting a self-effacing humor, in order to preserve social harmony.

	Individualist	Collectivist
Friendships	A wide range of social friends with whom one can interact, sometimes on a very occasional basis. Many friendships are a means to a particular end.	Few interpersonal relationships, but those one has are stable and long lasting and involve loyalty, obligations, and commitment.
Definition of Success	Self-made and can make up own mind; shows initiative and works well independently.	Works well within the group context, negotiates and even bends to the will of the majority.
Values	Believes that there are universal values that should be shared by all people.	Open to accepting that different groups have different values. One's own group is primary and thus sets the standard for moral values.
Child Rearing	Fosters independence in children by training them to think for themselves and by allowing them to make their own choices in many areas.	Fosters the development of group identities by teaching a child communal sensitivity and cooperation, and advising a child on all important matters.
Social Mobility	Values egalitarian relationships and flexibility in roles and recognizes that upward mobility should be available to all individuals.	Values stable hierarchical roles that are often dependent on gender, family background, age, and social rank.

	Individualist	**Collectivist**
Possessions	Values private property and individual ownership.	Recognizes shared property and group ownership.
Cultural Context	Lives in a low-context culture in which things are explicitly and concisely spelled out and one can depend on what is actually said or written. One is responsible to remain current in one's knowledge base and informal networks.	Lives in a high-context culture in which communication assumes a great deal of common knowledge and views. Much is communicated indirectly without being explicitly spelled out.

As a collectivist person Lydia was embedded in the wider society and cultural contexts in which she lived. In order to get to know her better we need to become familiar, not only with the details of her brief biography, but also with the relationships that she shared. In order to do this, we will look at key features of various aspects of Lydia's social world: the characteristics of the city in which she lived (chap. 1), the expectations and responsibilities she had as a householder (chap. 2), the perceptions that surrounded her whenever she entered into the public sphere of the marketplace (chap. 3), her networks as a businesswoman (chap. 4), and the religious roles she would have expected and been expected to play (chap. 5). With links to two urban centers (Thyatira and Philippi), and as a person who straddled two dominant cultures (Greek and Roman), not to mention her inscribed status as a woman who was working outside the home in the realm of men, Lydia was a "cosmopolitan" woman in the core sense of that word's meaning: one who is at home in diverse contexts. In examining these contexts we will not only come to understand Lydia better, she will provide for us a window into the lives of ancient Mediterranean women more generally. As such, we will discover a particular "sister in the faith" from the early Jesus groups, but, perhaps more important, we will discover typical characteristics of the many different women who comprised a significant part of Paul's social network.[9]

CHAPTER 1

Lydia in the Kolōnia

L ike many women and men in antiquity (and also today), Lydia inhabited two civic worlds. She was born and bred in the Asian city of Thyatira (in modern Turkey), but had moved at some point in her life to the Roman colony of Philippi (in Greek, *kolōnia*). And, like many immigrants, Lydia would have maintained aspects of her home culture, largely Greek and Eastern in nature, while adapting to and adopting many aspects of her new host culture, which was largely Roman—an irony, given that Philippi was in the northern part of the Greek-language homeland. In order to understand Lydia, we need to know a bit about her native and adoptive homes. Since she was living in Philippi at the time of her encounter with Paul, we will give more attention to the makeup of that particular city. In so doing, we are interested in forming generalizations, rather than outlining specific details, although some details will be important. We are aiming to understand what inhabitants of each city had in common.

Both Philippi and Thyatira were urban centers during the mid-first century. One thing is clear from studies of ancient life: urban centers were very different from rural locales, although how exactly urban centers were defined is difficult to determine. Richard Rohrbaugh points out that we have very little ancient evidence on which to draw for how the city was conceived among ancient persons. Pausanias, writing in the late second century CE, questions the status of Panopeus as a "city" by noting "if indeed one can give the name of city to those who possess no public buildings, no gymnasium, no theater, no market-place, no water descending to a fountain, but live in bare shelters just like mountain huts on the edges of ravines" (*Description of Greece* 10.4.1). Thus, public buildings rather than size of population define for Pausanias what constitutes a city. "By contrast, in his instructions for preparing an encomium to praise a city Menander Rhetor (*Epideictic Discourses*, Treatise I, 346–51) places far more emphasis on a city's 'origins, actions, and accomplishments' than he does on its location, size, or physical appearance."[1] It is the reputation of a city—its honor—that counts, which is confirmed by the inscriptional finds from many cities in which their own honor is proclaimed boldly for all to read.

It is also clear that the growth of cities in the late republic and early imperial periods reflected a shift in the relationship between cities and the surrounding rural areas. They were mutually dependent for their survival, with the countryside providing food for the city, and the city providing a market for rural produce. Nevertheless, urban inhabitants increasingly focused their attention inward to the status of their city, becoming ambivalent about the countryside. Ownership of the rural lands became concentrated in the hands of a few wealthy inhabitants of the city and as such provided these individuals with the economic means to display publicly their honor in the city. They may have built a large villa on their rural estates, but these functioned as extensions of the city, as owners would retreat there with a full entourage of family and slaves, and often entertained guests in the manner of civic banquets. Many rural folk remained on the land, but increasingly so as tenant farmers, or perhaps even slaves. Those who could not maintain such residency often joined the Roman military, becoming part of the apparatus that was meant to protect the empire, by which was largely meant the cities. Thus, despite the mutual dependency of one on the other, the urban centers had both the physical and social advantages.

Thyatira

In Acts 16:14 we learn that Lydia is from the city of Thyatira. No indication of when she moved to Philippi is given, although Luke does note that she is a merchant, which is a likely reason for her immigration to the city (see chap. 4). Her home city of Thyatira is located in an area in Asia Minor called Lydia (which may, as we noted above, be reflected in Lydia's name). Little is known about the city during the first century CE since few archaeological remains have been found at the site, much of which lies under the modern town of Akhisar. Archaeological evidence does show that the site was inhabited from around 3000 BCE, although of more interest is its coming under Greek influence through Alexander the Great at the end of the fourth century BCE. Subsequent control of the city was taken by the Seleucids, who refounded the city and settled it with Macedonian soldiers, making it a military outpost. Thyatira later came under the rule of the Pergamene kingdom, and thus came under Roman rule shortly after 133 BCE, when Attalus III bequeathed his kingdom to the Romans. Thus, the inhabitants were, like so many cities in the empire, truly Greco-Roman insofar as both cultures had impacted their local urban life. Many in Thyatira would, however, have traced their roots to Macedonian ancestors.

The city itself was situated at the crossroads of the major roads leading to and from the cities of Pergamum, Sardis, Magnesia, and Smyrna. This naturally caused the city to become an important center of trade and industry, with much commercial activity taking place. Evidence from inscriptions reveals the existence of a number of trade guilds, including bakers, potters or ceramists, tanners, leatherworkers, shoemakers, coppersmiths, and

Figure 2. The Scant Remains of Ancient Thyatira (photo by the author)

blacksmiths. The city was a particularly important center for the textile industry, as evidenced in a number of inscriptions mentioning wool workers, linen weavers, fullers, and dyers in and around Thyatira, guilds of the latter occupation being attested more than any others.[2]

Few architectural remains have been found at the site, but inscriptions show an active civic, social, and religious life during this period. Mention of shrines to Apollo Tyrimnaeus and Artemis Boreitene, to Helius, and to Hadrian give a sense of the deities worshiped. There also existed three gymnasiums full of statues, along with a large forum. During the Roman period the city was particularly prosperous, bolstered by its trade. Residents also took their marketing skills elsewhere, perhaps particularly with respect to the purple dye for which the region was justly famous (see chap. 4). Thus, we find in Thessalonica an inscription that names Menippus as a purple dealer from Thyatira, and we have the example of Lydia at Philippi. That a Jesus community developed at Thyatira is shown by the letter sent to the Jesus group there through the writer of the book of Revelation. Although they are praised for their love, faith, devotion, and good works, they are also censured for and called to repent from following the false teachings of "Jezebel," eating idol food, and engaging in immoral sexual practices (Rev 2:18-29).

Philippi

Although Thyatira was under Roman control and thus had a somewhat Roman cultural flavor to it, Philippi was much more of a Roman cultural center. According to Acts 16:15 Lydia had been settled in the city for some time, to the point of purchasing her own house (see chap. 2), which means that she was not a transient worker. As such, she would not only have carried with her customs from her home city but would very likely have adopted customs at Philippi itself. Since many commentators are convinced that the story of Lydia is historical, at least in broad outline, it is worth learning a bit more about the characteristics of her adopted city, and thus the cultural characteristics that she too would have needed to adopt in order to be enculturated into the city and succeed in her business venture there.

Philippi was located on the eastern border of what became the Roman province of Macedonia, strategically placed between the Strymon River to the west and the Nestos River to the east. A larger river, the Gangites, lay just over two kilometers from the city center, close to a commemorative arch, which marked the western edge of the sacred boundary of the city. Only sixteen kilometers (ten miles) inland from the Aegean Sea, Philippi was available as a frequent port of call for cargo ships.[3] The city was originally founded as Krenides by an Athenian exile named Callistratus, who brought with him a number of settlers from the island of Thasos (Strabo, *Geography*, VII, frags. 41, 42; Diodorus Siculus, *Library of History*, 16.3.7). Soon afterward, in 356

BCE, Philip II, the father of Alexander the Great, seized the city because of the gold and silver mines of Mount Pangaeus and renamed it after himself (Diodorus Siculus, *Library of History*, 16.3.6; 16.8.6-7). He increased the size of the city and settled a number of new inhabitants in it. He also seized Neapolis, a city likewise colonized by the people from nearby Thasos, to serve as the port for Philippi.

After the death of Alexander the Great in 332 BCE, political stability was never fully achieved in Macedonia until the arrival of the Romans in the mid-second century BCE. The Romans had begun to distrust the Macedonians and were attempting to block their expansion and meddle in their internal affairs. This led to a long and fierce battle between Perseus and the Romans. However, the Romans defeated Perseus at the Battle of Pydna in 168 BCE and gained control of the three important cities of Beroea, Thessalonica, and Pella. The area was not immediately annexed because the Senate decided that the Macedonians should be free, "so that it should be clear to all nations that the forces of the Roman people brought not slavery to free peoples but on the contrary, freedom to the enslaved" (Livy, *History of Rome*, 45.18.2, LCL). However, along with this "freedom" came an annual tribute paid to Rome, removal of all foreign possessions, and, most significantly, the division of Macedonia into four districts (Strabo, *Geography*, VII, frag. 47; Livy, *History of Rome*, 45.29.5-9). Each district was organized and governed autonomously, with a capital city in each. Land could not be sold across the boundaries and marriage was prohibited between people of different districts.

In 149 BCE Rome incorporated Macedonia into its empire by transforming it into a Roman province. The fourfold division of the area remained, as did the general laws already in place, but each part was treated as a single unit, with a Roman governor, and accompanying legions, permanently installed at Thessalonica. Many Roman veterans were settled in the regions where they had fought and many chose to remain there after demobilization. Organized colonization began after Julius Caesar, with the first cities being Kassandreia and Dion (43/42 BCE), followed by Philippi shortly thereafter. Under Augustus Macedonia was made a senatorial province.

In the civil unrest that followed the murder of Julius Caesar, the climactic battle between the forces of Brutus and Cassius and the forces of Octavian and Antony took place on the plain to the west of Philippi (42/41 BCE), with Octavian and Antony emerging as victors. Antony settled his veterans there and renamed the city *Antoni Iussu Colonia Victrix Philippensium* to commemorate his victory. Eleven years after their battle with Brutus and Cassius, Octavian defeated Antony at the Battle of Actium, and there was a fresh influx of immigrants into Philippi. This was a mixture of Octavian's own veterans along with Italian supporters of Antony who had to give up their Italian lands to supporters of Octavian (Dio Cassius, *Roman History*, 51.4.6). The new name of the city was *Colonia Iulia Augusta Philippensis*, indicating its new status as a Roman colony.

During the *pax Romana* (the Roman peace) new cities were founded in Macedonia, especially under Augustus and Tiberius. These included settlements of Roman veterans (*coloniae*) and native settlements granted urban autonomy (*municipia*). At that time, older cities were remodeled following new plans, and grand building projects were undertaken, including agoras, temples, altars, and funerary buildings, all with accompanying inscriptions. A detailed history of Macedonia during the imperial period is not well known. A number of emperors passed through the province on their way to or from some eastern campaign, and it continued to be an important political stronghold in the third century CE and through the time of Constantine the Great.

As a Roman colony Philippi was granted the honor of *ius italicum*, the "Italian law," which meant that it was treated as if it were on Italian soil. This gave it equal status with other Italian cities, and it was governed by Roman law and was free from any kind of direct taxation on its lands or citizens. The city's constitution would have been modeled on the municipal constitution of Rome, and it had two collegiate magistrates governing it, a fact reflected in Luke's use of *stratēgoi* (equal to *duo uiri* or *duumvirs*,

Acts 16:35, 36, 38). Even the pattern of the city and the style and architecture of the buildings were copied from Rome. Not only Roman in law and in style, it was also Roman in ethos, since many of the residents at Philippi were veterans, presumably from Italy.

When the writer of Acts notes that Philippi was a Roman colony, using the transliterated Latin term *kolōnia*, he is entirely correct. Not so is his designation of Philippi as a "first city of the district of Macedonia" (16:12). As we noted above, Macedonia was a Roman province, not a "district," and the capital city, or "first" city, of the province was Thessalonica, wherein the proconsul resided. The Greek manuscripts for this verse reflect the problem and attest to different attempts to provide a correction for Luke's mistake. Even the recent editions of the Greek New Testament make an emendation to the text, with no basis at all in the manuscript tradition, in order to make Luke's description conform to the historical situation and read "a city of the first district of Macedonia." The lack of evidence for this reading has caused some to maintain the most widely attested reading—"a first city of the district of Macedonia"—and find an alternative explanation. Drawing on a wide range of evidence for expressions of intercity rivalry and civic pride, I have argued in detail elsewhere that by referring to Philippi as a first or leading city Luke's eyewitness source writer is expressing his pride in what is likely his hometown.[4] It may not be historically accurate, but it expresses a common sentiment in an honor/shame culture, one that finds analogy today in the expression at sporting events when fans of a team call out "NN is number one," when the city of NN is neither the federal nor state capital (and more often than not is not even in first place in that particular sport!).

During the republican period the Romans built a major road, the Via Egnatia, across Macedonia from the Adriatic coast to the Aegean Sea, over eight hundred kilometers in length. It served as a main artery for military and civilian traffic through the province and led to a resurgence of the economic life in Macedonia during the Roman period. This highway was the main

Figure 3. Overview of the Forum at Philippi (photo by Rachel McRae, used with permission)

thoroughfare for people, goods, and troops moving between Rome and its eastern provinces, and it ran through the center of Philippi, bringing to the inhabitants there many of the same goods that were produced by and for Rome. Coming up to the city from the port of Neapolis, Paul would have entered the city through the so-called Neapolis Gate on the east side of the city, having passed through the east cemetery. It was likely through one of the gates on the other side of the city, however, that Paul sought the "place of prayer" (Greek *proseuchē*), near a small stream just outside the western wall, but not as far as the Gangites River a few kilometers further west (see site plan, fig. 1).[5]

The city grid and the architectural style of the buildings at Philippi were copied from Rome, although admittedly most of the archaeological finds date from the second century CE or later. Latin was the official language of the colony during the Julio-Claudian period, and most of the inscriptions found to date are in Latin. Yet this was the public face of the city, and Greek remained the language used for common communication,[6] as was the case in many Roman cities in the eastern part of the empire. Overall, the historical and architectural background point to the distinctive Latin character of Philippi, where Roman culture predominated. This will become a key issue when we examine the type of behavior and attitudes that would have been expressed by and about Lydia, as a resident of the city.

Writing in the early part of the second century CE, Aulus Gellius commented that Roman colonies

> were transplanted from the State and have all the laws and institutions of the Roman people, not those of their own choice. This condition, although it is more exposed to control and less free, is nevertheless thought preferable and superior because of the greatness and majesty of the Roman people, of which those colonies seem to be miniatures, as it were, and in a way copies. (*Attic Nights* 16.13.8-9)

As Hellerman notes, "the comments are particularly apropos for Philippi, since epigraphic data demonstrates unequivocally that the colony was administrated by Romans in a decidedly Roman fashion."[7] Although archaeological excavations have turned up Hellenistic streets under the currently exposed Roman streets in some areas of the city, during the mid-first century the city would have been quite Roman in ethos. Both Augustus and Claudius had introduced building programs that changed the face of the city, although today much of their building has been obliterated by the building projects of later emperors Antoninus Pius and Justinian. During Paul's time the central forum contained statues of the emperor Augustus and his family, along with monuments to other members of the imperial family. The city witnessed the establishment of the cult of Augustus and his adopted sons Gaius and Lucius Caesar, and the cult of Livia, wife of Augustus and mother of Tiberius. Numismatic and archaeological evidence from the founding of Philippi as a colony explicitly identify Philippi with Augustus and the empire he had begun to construct. Further, "inscriptions left by the veteran colonists consistently attest to their loyalty to Rome and her emperor, and also to the pride taken by these soldiers in their former positions of honor in the army."[8]

The social makeup of the population of Philippi developed over the course of three stages: "initial occupation of land by the colonists; spread of colonial land to distant parts of the territory; concentration of land ownership."[9] Land became concentrated in the hands of a few persons, since land ownership was the main indicator of wealth, causing the majority of the population to move to the city, where power and benefaction by the elite predominated. The general pattern of development suggests that by the mid-first century the majority of the population of the town was probably neither Romans nor citizens and the overall proportion of veterans was negligible. Most likely there was a proportion of 30% Romans to 50% non-slave Greeks over-all in the first-century city. Of these, the term "Romans" repre-sents all citizens and their families, while the term "Greeks" subsumes all Greek-speaking persons such as Thracians, Mace-donians, Asians, and the like—in other words, noncitizen Greek speakers. Another 20% of the population was comprised of Greek slaves, who were largely the property of the Romans.[10]

Using population density data from other cities in the empire and relating it to the urban area and the surrounding countryside under its control, Oakes estimates the population of Philippi at around fifteen thousand in the mid-first century CE.[11] The result-ing distribution of the population of the city during the middle of the first century gives a picture of a very small percentage of the population with the status of Roman elite, perhaps 1.5–5 %, with another 7% representing the slaves of this group. Commut-ing peasant colonists, half of them land owners and half renters, represented 20–30% , with an additional 5% for their slaves. By far the largest social level was represented by the service groups, at 30–45%, three-quarters of them Greek, the others Roman. The Romans in this category would have also had slaves, comprising about 8%. Finally, the urban poor comprised about 15–30% of the population, with Greeks occupying about 70% of this rank and Romans filling in the remaining 30%. Using Oakes' notional figures for the city, we get the following distribution of the total population:

Percentage Distribution of Population of Philippi			
	Romans	Greeks	Slaves of
Roman Elite	3%	0%	7%
Commuting Peasant Colonists	10%	10%	5%
Service Groups	9%	28%	8%
Poor	6%	14%	0%
Total (of 100%)	28%	52%	20%

Numeric Distribution of Population of Philippi			
	Romans	Greeks	Slaves of
Roman Elite	450	0	1,050
Commuting Peasant Colonists	1,500	1,500	750
Service Groups	1,350	4,200	1,200
Poor	900	2,100	0
Total (of 15,000 persons)	4,200	7,800	3,000

The percentages need not be exact, and the numeric distribution numbers would be smaller had we used Pilhofer's smaller population estimate, but these charts give us a general picture of the overall distribution of the social ranks at Philippi, and we can see that Lydia would have fit into the largest of these social ranks, Greek-speaking workers in the service industry: 28% of the population, or around 4,200 persons.

As the city of Philippi was colonized and grew, previous local landholders were displaced from their land by elite landowners who lived in the city. As a consequence, those who stayed in the area, of which there were quite a number, moved to the city.

Peasant colonists, rather than locals, were employed by the new elite Roman landowners in order to work the land. As for the local Greek elite, there is no evidence for their persistence beyond the time of colonization, suggesting that they either lost their status or moved to other cities.[12] The native population of non-Romans, those in the city and those displaced from the countryside, would have then become the core of the service industries in Philippi, a need for which increased substantially with the arrival of the colonists. An increase in the construction of luxury items such as monuments attests to the increase in wealth among the new elite, and a desire to expend that wealth on displays of honor, which would have necessitated more and more service personnel, not only slaves, but also day workers and contract workers. "One effect of this demand, particularly in the area of specialist luxury goods such as purple, was the drawing in of further merchants and craftspeople from other regions, in particular Asia."[13] Thus, we discover in the study of the demographic changes in the city a plausible reason why we find Lydia and her household in Philippi at the time of Paul's visit.

Clearly, Lydia was neither a veteran nor even a Roman, being an immigrant from the city of Thyatira, and thus likely of Greek background. Nevertheless, as we have seen, her hometown was impacted by the presence of Rome in the land, as was her adopted home, to an even greater degree. As Hellerman sums up of Philippi, "Though a numerical minority, the Romans remained an ideological majority, particularly where issues of honor, status, and social values were concerned, since the dispossession of local landholders by Roman veterans ultimately determined not only the social hierarchy, but also the social values, of the reconstituted settlement."[14] How and why this Romanization of Philippi took place we will examine in the next chapter, giving particular attention to the impact that it would have had on women such as Lydia. This generalized picture will allow us to draw some conclusions about the economic and marital status of Lydia herself.

CHAPTER 2

Lydia in the Household

Whereas in the modern world we generally divide the stages of life similarly for men and women along the lines of infancy, childhood, adolescence, adulthood, and old age, in antiquity life was marked separately for the genders. For women, the key biological and social markers in life, assuming they survived infancy, were puberty, marriage, childbirth, and, for those few who survived long enough, menopause. The central marker of transformation for a woman in antiquity was the transfer of her care from her father to her husband—in both cases she did not achieve her autonomy, a fact of her existence throughout her life. There were some exceptions to this, however, which we will explore further below, as they have implications for our understanding of Lydia.

Acts 16:40 notes Lydia's place in the formation of the Philippian Jesus group. It is at her house that Paul and Silas encourage the brothers and sisters before leaving the city (Acts 16:40). The Greek word used, *adelphoi*, is literally "brothers," but here cannot be that gender specific since this Jesus group was a women's group at its core (see also the women mentioned in Phil 4:2-3). Thus, Luke indicates that Lydia allowed her house to be used as the meeting place of the initial Jesus devotees at Philippi (Acts 16:15). There are some curious aspects to the scenario, however, not least of which is Lydia's ability to act independently of a male guardian and the indication of *her* household, whereas the expectation would have been that the household was designated in the name of her legal male guardian. In this chapter, we will look at two aspects of Lydia's social location in the household—her status as householder and her marital status. We will then note some implications of our conclusions in terms of Lydia's ability to provide hospitality, first to Paul and his companions and then to a wider body of believers, and her ability to be a patron.

Lydia's Household

The Greek word Luke uses at Acts 16:15 for "house," *oikos*, and its synonym, *oikia*, can indicate an actual house or simply one's dwelling. The question is whether the reference to Lydia's *oikos* indicates a separate *domus* (house), a larger building that could incorporate a number of inhabitants, or an apartment in an *insula*, a commercial block of flats, which would accommodate her extended family but not much more. If one assumes Lydia was wealthy, then a *domus* is more likely; assuming she was poor places her in an *insula*. Unfortunately, this is a chicken-egg problem and linguistically there is not much help from the word *oikos* itself. We can, however, examine how Luke uses this word in his gospel and Acts to see whether that will shed any light.

Once one removes references to the "house of God" or the "house of" one of the Hebrew Bible patriarchs, most of the uses of *oikos/oikia* in Luke-Acts refer to the physical building in which persons dwell. The majority of these references refer to independently owned or rented houses of some size—that is, to a *domus* rather than an *insula*. For example, the centurion whose slave has fallen ill lives in a house (Luke 7:6, 10) as does his counterpart in Acts, Cornelius, who has disposable income and a large domestic staff (Acts 10:2, 22, 30; 11:12-14). Various Jewish leaders also live in houses of some size, as suggested by their ability to host banquets (Pharisees in Luke 7:36, 37; 14:1) or the presence of multiple rooms (Jairus in Luke 8:41, 51) or a courtyard (the high priest's house, Luke 22:54-55). Tax collectors, notorious for their wealth, are also indicated as owning houses (Levi in Luke 5:29; the repentant sinner in Luke 18:14; Zacchaeus in Luke 19:5). When teaching in parables, Jesus uses *oikos* to refer to the houses of the wealthy (the ill-attended banquet in Luke 14:23; the forgiving father in Luke 15:25; the dishonest manager in Luke 16:4; the rich man and Lazarus in Luke 16:20, 27), or at least those who own more valuable property than most of their neighbors could afford (one hundred sheep in Luke 15:4 or ten silver coins Luke 15:8).

Of even more interest to us in terms of identifying the use of *oikos* relating to Lydia is Luke's use of *oikos/oikia* with reference to those who hosted the early Jesus believers. At the climax of the gospel narrative Luke notes that Jesus directs his disciples to procure a location for his final Passover meal in the large furnished guest room of a house owner, who has at least one slave (Luke 22:10-11). As the book of Acts opens, we again find the disciples gathered in a large house, one that can accommodate at least 120 people (Acts 1:15; 2:1). Among the early Jesus believers in Jerusalem are some who own houses, at least until they sell them to share the proceeds with others (Acts 4:34). While in Caesarea Maritima, Peter lodges with a tanner named Simon, "whose house is by the seaside" (Acts 10:6, 32; 11:11) and is protected by a gate (10:17), as was the custom for the houses of the wealthy. Because Simon has a low occupation—he works with leather and, of necessity, with urine for curing the leather—it is striking that he owns his own gated house. In Jerusalem, Mary, the mother of John Mark, owns her own house, again noted as being gated, and has at least one domestic slave (Acts 12:12-13).

Once Paul experiences the risen Jesus we find him staying "at the house of Judas" in Damascus (Acts 9:11, cf. 9:17), a pattern of household accommodation that continues through the narrative. Bypassing the Lydia narrative for the moment, but remaining at Philippi, we note that Paul and Silas are brought into the house of the jailer, where they share a meal with the newly believing members of the household (Acts 16:32, 34). In Thessalonica Paul and Silas are offered hospitality by Jason, who owns his own house where he and other believers have met, including "not a few of the leading women," a reference to the well-to-do (Acts 17:4-7). In Corinth Paul first stays with a married couple, Aquila and Priscilla, with whom he shares the same trade and alongside whom he works at that trade (Acts 18:2-4; Priscilla also goes by the name Prisca—see Rom 16:3; 1 Cor 16:19; 2 Tim 4:19). Where they are living is not mentioned and the use of *oikos/oikia* is strikingly absent, leading one to assume they are in a tenement building (*insula*). When his companions, Silas and Timothy, arrive from Macedonia, Paul moves to stay with Titius Justus, whose "house [*oikos*] was next door to the synagogue" (Acts 18:7); no reason is given for this switch except Paul's rejection by the members of the synagogue and his decision to "go to the Gentiles" (18:6). Paul remains friends with his initial Jewish hosts, Aquila and Priscilla, since they later accompany him from Corinth to Ephesus (18:18, 26), so clearly they were not among the *Ioudaioi* who rejected Paul.[1] One can conjecture that the reason Paul needed to move to Titius Justus' house was the need for more space to accommodate his recently arrived companions—Aquila and Priscilla's dwelling was simply not large enough, as would have been the case for most artisans. In subsequent locales Paul continues the pattern of teaching in houses (Acts 20:20, cf. 19:16) and staying in such (Acts 21:8).

We can now return to the case of Lydia and the writer's mention of her *oikos* in Acts 16:15. The references examined above suggest some precedents for understanding that Lydia was the owner of her own house, in which she dwelt with her wider household. Luke certainly knows that some people in the service industry, among whom we can place Lydia the purple dealer, could own their own houses, as in the case of Simon the tanner in Caesarea Maritima (Acts 10:6), in contradistinction to Aquila and Priscilla in Corinth (Acts 18:2-4). Certainly we have an example of a woman who owns her own house and has at least one slave in the story of Mary, the mother of John Mark (Acts 12:12-13). Lydia's story is also bracketed with the stories of two men, both of whom carry a designation similar to Lydia as a "fearer of God" or a "worshiper of God" and both of whom own their own houses: Cornelius the Centurion in Caesarea Maritima (Acts 10:2) and Titius Justus in Corinth (Acts 18:7). Finally, Luke draws attention on a few occasions to women of wealth and status as being at the core of the early Jesus groups in other Macedonian cities such as Thessalonica (Acts 17:4) and Beroea (17:12). Thus, we can conclude that Luke is portraying Lydia as a woman of means who owns her own house.

Just what sort of house the ancient reader would imagine is difficult to determine, although archaeology can "help us understand the social, cultural, and religious environment of the households in which families in Pauline churches lived and worshipped."[2] Unfortunately, due to ill-preservation and underfunded excavations, the archaeological remains currently visible at Philippi are not particularly great. Unlike extensively excavated sites such as Corinth, Rome, Pompeii, or Ephesus, we know little about the domestic architecture and decoration at Philippi. This makes it difficult to ascertain just what to imagine when Luke tells us that Lydia invites Paul and his companions to her house (Acts 16:15) and later that there is a gathering of Jesus devotees in that same house (Acts 16:40). Here we must again undertake an exercise of disciplined imagination in order to construct how an ancient reader might have understood Luke's narrative.

It has been suggested that Lydia was operating her own business and had a "household" with her. Lydia's household could have been comprised not only of immediate family members such as children, but also of extended family members (e.g., cousins, in-laws), slaves, freed persons employed in her business, and even some of the urban poor, for whom Lydia may have been a patron. Recent studies have suggested that the "standard image of the Roman *domus* as a 'single-family unit'" has given way to an image of "a 'big house' inhabited by a 'houseful' rather than a household; not only a parent-children-slaves unit, but a cluster linked by relationships that could vary from relationship and dependency to commercial tenancy."[3] Should this be the case for Lydia, she would have been a woman of some means.

This is certainly how Luke presents other (unnamed) Macedonian women who come to believe in Jesus (Acts 17:4, 12), so Lydia falls into this pattern. That said, we can rule out a scenario in which Lydia dwelt in a rented domicile such as a tenement building (*insula*). She may have lived in a small house on a busy street full of shops. In this case, her ground floor would have functioned as her storefront, with an upper floor or two serving as the living quarters. Such dwellings, though common, were not likely, however, for a woman of means. More likely is the assumption that she dwelt in a reasonably sized *domus* or "atrium house." Although there is little clear archaeological evidence concerning private dwellings in Philippi during the time of Lydia, some excavation done in the eastern part of the city has revealed a number of large houses, leading Chaido Koukouli-Chrysantaki to conclude that Lydia's house "must have been a large building, like the late Roman and early Christian houses recently excavated."[4]

For our purposes, we can look elsewhere for an understanding of what such a house might have entailed. This is justified, in the minds of many archaeologists and biblical scholars, by noting that housing in Roman cities (of which Philippi was one) tended to be "typical"—that is, patterns of housing were replicated, at least so far as we can discern from comparing housing in various places. It is also likely that various types of housing existed alongside one another, with tenements adjacent to larger atrium houses, as was the case in Rome.[5] Two Roman cities that have undergone extensive archaeological excavation and provide fitting analogies for imagining how Philippian houses, particularly Lydia's house, might have looked are Pompeii and Ephesus.

Using such points of comparison, since Lydia was able to accommodate not only her immediate household but also the visiting preachers, we can estimate that she lived in at least a medium-sized house. Like many of her contemporaries, she may have redesigned her house, or, more likely, purchased one already so redesigned, to "include a peristyle courtyard with as many impressive reception and dining rooms around the courtyard as possible, decorated with real or imitation marble, thereby identifying themselves with the Roman way of life (13, 21, 117)."[6] Walls would have been plastered and decorated with paintings depicting pastoral scenes, realistic window views, mythological stories, and such. Floors were likewise richly decorated, often employing mosaic tile to depict scenes.

That women could own such houses is attested by a number of archaeological remains, not least of which is the case of a woman named Julia Felix, who owned one of the largest Pompeiian residences (Region II, insula iv), which included baths, taverns, shops, and second story rooms. "We may realistically imagine her in the *tablinum* (office) of her house advising clients, freedmen, and slaves operating shops in her house, at her baths, or managing her extensive gardens."[7]

As a householder, Lydia would have been similar to others who hosted Jesus groups in their houses and who

> typically would have internalized the values and aspirations of those who were wealthy. In the climate of competition in Greco-Roman society, "everything the upper classes did was imitated" (141). "In a competitive society with relatively extensive upward mobility, the powerful create models for less wealthy and powerful contemporaries through their habits and the style in which they live, at least when they place themselves on display as ostentatiously as Roman aristocrats did" (13).[8]

Lydia would have had a *lararium*, a small shrine, usually located inside the house or in the garden. It was the place where the family prayed on a daily basis, perhaps offering small gifts such as fruit or wine, to the *Lares* (the household spirits), to Vesta (goddess of the hearth), and to the *genius* (the guardian spirit of the family). Images—either statuettes, reliefs, or paintings—included any number of motifs and one often finds pastoral motifs, depictions of gods and goddesses, scenes from myths, one or more *Lares* holding a drinking horn and cup, or the family in worship. If, as some argue, Lydia was already a worshiper of the Israelite God, presumably her *lararium* would have stood empty, a reminder of the prohibition against graven images. On the other hand, if, as I will argue in chapter 5, Lydia still retained ritual practices typical of those outside of Judaism, then the *lararium* would have immediately identified for any visitors to her house, including Paul, something of Lydia's *pietas*, her devotion. The *lararium*, along with wall paintings and other household decorations displayed to the public—visitors, clients, even passersby—the stories or images that the householder found most significant.[9]

Lydia's Marital Status

In the Greco-Roman world individualism was rare, and a person's identity and purpose were unquestionably embedded in his or her roles within the family and within the household's role in the wider community—what was described in the introduction as a collectivist culture. In contrast to the modern Western notion of family as a fairly small, tight-knit unit of horizontal relationships grounded in love and caring, the ancient understanding of family was grounded in vertical relations of power, dependence, and subordination. Family households fell under the authority of the oldest living male relative, who was considered the "father of the household," the *paterfamilias*. As such, "he had in his paternal power (*patria potestas*) his children and remoter descendants in the male line (grandchildren by sons, great-grandchildren by grandsons, but not his daughter's children, and so on)" and could expect from them obedience to his will.[10] Also under his authority were domestic slaves, slaves purchased as craft-producers (if the *paterfamilias* was a manufacturer), former slaves who had become clients, any hired agricultural laborers (slave or free) living on his land, and sometimes business associates or tenants. This is what is meant by a "patriarchal society"—it is a socio-cultural system in which a few men have power over other men, women, children, slaves, and colonized people. In a patri-archal system women generally had a lower status, and it is in such a patriarchal society that we must locate Lydia. As we shall see, however, during Lydia's lifetime there were some social forces at work that made it *relatively* easier (that is, to a small degree) for women to have a bit of independence.

Within this patriarchal system, the ancient (male) under-standing of physiology was very different from that of today. A brief review can help modern readers understand (but not agree with) why women were subjugated at that time. Although not unheard of, autopsies and dissection of the human body were rare in antiquity, leaving knowledge of the inner workings of the body to what could be observed due to injuries or battle wounds. We have little remaining from the ancient physicians themselves, although an early second-century physician named Galen did record much of the extant medical knowledge. His views on the differences between males and females are particu-larly instructive for understanding some of the reasons women were assumed to be different, in fact inferior, to men.

According to Galen, a woman's reproductive system is an inverted replica of the male genitalia. It is this inversion that causes her weakness and hence her inferiority—she is unable to project the inner parts outward. This is confirmed by her com-parative lack of physical strength. At the same time, there was a general (male) fear about a woman's menstrual cycle. "A woman's ability to bleed without injury and the association of her monthly periods with fertility rendered menstruation mys-terious to men, which generated concepts of pollution."[11] In all societies systems of meaning and taxonomies of placement are brought into being. People organize their worlds in a way that will make sense out of human existence. Within such a system things are either in their proper place or out of place. These bifurcated points often translate into categories of what is pure or clean (in place) and what is impure, polluted, or unclean (out of place). Although socially constructed, such labels are given biological or natural justifications, as is the case with Galen's attempt to explain the differences between males and females. Once males are defined as normative any deviation from the norm can be labeled out of place or impure. This was one key justification for the systemic relegation of women to a secondary position vis-à-vis men.

Another key factor in the social construction of a purity system consists of contrasting what belongs and what does not belong, but in terms of internalization and externalization around certain boundaries. That which belongs inside is considered pure, whereas that which is outside of something is considered dirty and thus is impure. Physical manifestations of a skin disease, so-called leprosy, for example, becomes like dirt, making those inflicted and anyone who touches them unclean (and thus taboo). Blood belongs inside the body, so that those who inexplicably have an external flow of blood on a regular basis, namely women, are designated in the system as unclean during that time. Such persons were avoided as contact transferred the dirt and defiled the one touching. Yet there is also a situatedness of the system that allows defilement in one context to be acceptable in another—contact with blood, for example, may pollute if the blood originates from a woman's menstrual cycle but not if it comes from the engagement with one's enemies during battle.

Such systems also provide mechanisms of restoration, with everything from simple to elaborate rituals and short or lengthy temporal periods of isolation designated to bring a person back into a state of purity. The Israelite purity system is well known to many students of the Bible, with lengthy and seemingly complex governance around what is and is not pure and how restoration is to take place through ritual. A reading of the books of

Leviticus or Numbers in light of anthropological and sociological understandings of purity systems begins to clarify the internal logic within the system itself. Systems of purity and pollution were also in place in the Greek and Roman worlds, not perhaps as elaborate as that of the Israelites but nevertheless important, particularly in cultic contexts. For example, a first-century BCE inscription from a house-based cult-group in the Asia Minor city of Philadelphia stipulates a number of restrictions on men and women in order to keep pure the rituals of the group:

> A free woman is to be chaste and shall not know the bed of another man, except her own husband, nor have intercourse. But if she should know the bed of another, such a woman is not chaste, but defiled and full of pollution of the kinsmen, and unworthy to worship this god whose holy things these are that have been set up, nor is she to be present at the sacrifices, nor to strike against the purifications and cleansings, nor to see the mysteries being performed. (*SIG*[3rd ed.] 985)

Women could become unclean not only through touching certain items (a dead body; swine; garlic!) as could men, but also through menstruation and childbirth. Because of these latter items women were especially unclean and were to be avoided.

Given the perceived inferiority of women in general, individual women were unquestionably assumed to need the guidance and protection of a male: "The weakness and light-mindedness of the female sex (*infirmitas sexus* and *levitas animi*) were the underlying principles of Roman legal theory that mandated all women be under the custody of males."[12] This was the function of the *paterfamilias* in the life of his wife, mother, sisters, daughters, nieces, and female clients. He would serve as the guardian, known in Greek as the *kyrios*, or he would appoint an appropriate male *kyrios* for each woman who fell into his orbit of authority. This *kyrios*, whether the *paterfamilias* or another male relative such as an uncle, son, or brother, acted on behalf of the women in his care in all legal and public exchanges. For any such transactions to take place without the presence of a *kyrios* would have branded the woman involved as shameless and would have brought dishonor to the *paterfamilias* and his family. "Thus, if a woman appears (e.g., Lydia, Acts 16:13-15) who is not identified as the wife of so-and-so, the reader would be expected to wonder as to her 'shame,' that is, her defense of feminine sexual exclusivity and family virtue."[13]

One of the benefits of living under such guardianship was the protection it afforded to women, not only physically but also publicly through the protection of her status. For example, a male child remained with his mother until puberty; afterward he remained as his mother's ally and advocate of her interests within the family (sometimes resisting his own father, wife, father's family, etc.). Likewise, a woman's brothers would have looked out for her, becoming highly incensed when any unauthorized male approached a sister. If a daughter misbehaved sexually, the father would have held her responsible (for being "shameless") whereas her brother would have sought out the offending party and attempted revenge (cf. 2 Sam 13:1-29, Tamar and her stepbrother). Nevertheless, the overall impact proved very restrictive for women, whose relationship with men tended toward subordination, and they were the object of constant surveillance, to the point where, according to one ancient writer, "women were customarily kissed on the mouth by their male blood relations in order to determine if they had alcohol on their breath."[14]

Another consequence of the patriarchal structures of ancient society was the relegation of women to the domestic sphere. Yet it is within this domestic sphere that women established their identity and found some sources of power. Inside the home the wife of the *paterfamilias* ran many aspects of the household and had some say in what took place on a daily basis. Yet this was a limited source for identity, as it was comprised largely of domestic duties such as childcare, food preparation, housecleaning, fulfilling household rituals, conducting or supervising all cloth production, and gathering fuel (usually wood) and water—in a nutshell, "chores usually relegated to servants and slaves."[15] An inscribed eulogy on a grave from the time of Augustus records an elite husband's praise for his wife, which includes the following:

> Why should I recall your domestic qualities—your chastity, obedience, graciousness, amiability, zeal in wool-working, piety without superstition, your unostentatious dress, your modest adornment? Why should I speak of your affection, your duty to family (*pietas familiae*), since you devoted yourself just as much to my mother as to your own parents and you cultivated the same tranquility with her as with them—and other innumerable qualities which you had in common with all matrons who enjoy a worthy reputation?[16]

This eulogy, although highly personal, was composed for public reading, and as such presents for us a window on the values of the composer and his society. In a similar vein, a Roman tomb inscription from around 135–120 BCE expresses the values of the time:

> Stranger, my message is short. Stand by and read it through. Here is the unlovely tomb of a lovely woman. Her parents called her Claudia by name. She loved her husband with all her heart. She bore two sons; of these she leaves one on earth; under the earth she has placed the other. She was charming in converse, yet gentle in bearing. She kept house, she made wool. That's my last word. Go your way.[17]

Claudia, according to her epitaph, did all that was required of a proper matron, and crossed no socially scripted boundaries.

Bruce W. Winter summarizes the *status quo* position of women's lives during the late republic and early empire by noting that "heads of some households could hold total sway over their wives, making them subject to their husband's domination and their position vulnerable to exploitation."[18] The social and legal constrictions on women made it difficult for them to engage in business on their own, initiate lawsuits or answer to charges in courts, or make their own marital arrangements or other decisions about their lives. Nevertheless, there was more to women's lives in the first century CE than this restrictive picture. To understand how and why some women in the first century could navigate the public sphere on their own, women such as Lydia, we need to look at first-century views on marriage and the reforms to family life introduced by the emperor Augustus.

In the Greco-Roman period, marriage was set up on a contractual basis by the parents of the couple. These carefully negotiated arrangements between two extended families represented a fusion of the honor of the two extended families. The bride's family looked for a groom who would be a good provider, a kind father, and a respected citizen, while the family of the groom looked for a bride of good breeding, with a substantial dowry, and the promise of children to extend the patrilineal line. The bride and groom did not look to one another for companionship or comfort—that came from siblings and friends; in the case of the bride, women friends. Often the couple did not know one another beforehand, although they most likely came from within the same wider kinship group or village. This practice, known as endogamy, was common in the ancient circum-Mediterranean world (and remains common in many cultures today). More typical in North American cultures today are exogamous marriages, wherein marriages take place across kinship groups, classes, or ethnicities. Endogamous marriages served to tighten the inner-kinship bonds and keep honor within the kinship group.

Within marriage a wife was expected to obey her husband in all things, and her primary role was childbearing and child rearing. Sex was for the purpose of procreation (particularly of male heirs), and, given the risks to a woman of pregnancy and childbirth, sex for pleasure was not undertaken, at least not with one's wife. Many males relied on prostitutes, concubines, slaves, or homoerotic encounters for recreational sex. The purpose of marriage is explained as follows:

> Because marriage was not a religious concern in most
> ancient cultures, there was not any religious sanction for

marriage, but weddings publicly marked the community's recognition of the couple's new status as husband and wife. This new status entailed the couple's readiness to establish a household together, to bear and raise children, and to perform their respective civic and religious obligations.[19]

Nevertheless, many marriages were not without love, or even passion, as attested in the epitaphs and engraved reliefs found at many ancient gravesites.

For many ancient families the birth of a girl was viewed as a liability. As she grew older she needed to be furnished with a dowry, and she could not have been expected to be employed in the family business. Many husbands decided either not to have further children once a male heir had been born, or, if a female baby was born, to expose the child in the hopes that it would die or be picked up by a slave trader. As a result, during the reign of the emperor Augustus there was a perceived crisis in that the population of freeborn, freed persons, and citizens was not reproducing at a rate that would keep the overall population constant or growing. The insufficient number of females for purposes of marriage and procreation led Augustus to introduce legislation that "regulated marriage, encouraged procreation by privileges and rewards, and penalized the unmarried and childless, in particular restricting their rights of inheritance."[20] Functionally, these laws, which were intended to preserve the old republican ideals of family life, served to provide some women with more relative freedoms than were hitherto available to them.

Under the older marriage legislation a daughter would normally have been married according to the legal marriage contract with *manus*, which meant that she was released from the authority of her father, and transferred to the power (*manus*) of her husband, becoming part of her husband's family and subject to the *paterfamilias* of her husband's household.[21] This included property rights, which meant that her dowry, supplied by her own father, was now the full possession of her husband's family.

Should they divorce, the dowry would have remained with her husband. The bride also gave up her father's, and thus her, ancestral cultic practices and took on the ancestors, guardian spirits, and public religious practices of her husband's family.

As an alternative, the bride's *paterfamilias* could have decided that his daughter would be married without *manus* (known as *sine manu*). In such a case, a woman remained under the authority of her own father or a *kyrios*, and her husband retained no legal authority over her, or her property. A woman's property was kept separate from her husband's property and she could inherit her father's property upon his death. In the Augustan Age divorce could have been initiated by either party for a variety of reasons, and thus divorce was common, especially in light of *sine manu* marriage laws, which allowed the return of the wife's property to her father's household. Nevertheless, either with or without *manus* a woman remained under male guardianship of one sort or another.

The Augustan legislation provided a means for women to be liberated from the legal supervision of a male *kyrios*. Two laws, the *lex Iulia de maritandis ordinibus* (18 BCE) and the *lex Papia Poppaea* (9 CE), gave a number of rights to women who were freeborn or freed. One particular aspect of the law, commonly referred to as the *ius (trium) liberorum* exempted free women who had borne three sons and freedwomen who had borne four sons from certain taxes and from the need to act through their legal male *kyrios*—they were considered to be of such moral fiber in birthing these children (and surviving!) that they were deemed capable of enacting legal and financial transactions of their own accord.[22] Such legislation allowed some women to attain a fair degree of autonomy, particularly if they were divorced or widowed. These Roman legal formulations and the marriage values that they entailed spread rapidly into the eastern regions of the empire, and thus influenced women in most urban centers, particularly those that had become heavily Romanized.[23]

Mortality rates from antiquity are not easy to determine, particularly since the records we have are rather sketchy and are localized. The attempts that have been made paint a picture of life expectancies that are rather bleak. Although much of the evidence comes from the late Roman period and/or from Egypt, it is probably safe to assume that the overall conditions across the empire in the first century were not particularly better. We find that there was a very high infant mortality rate, especially up to age one, assuming the child even made it past the threats of miscarriage and stillbirth. One third of those who survived infancy were dead by age six and half of the children died by age ten. Nearly 60% of these survivors died by age sixteen and by age twenty-six 75% were dead. By age forty-six 90% had passed away, and less than 3% of the population made it to age sixty. According to estimates drawn from Roman Egypt, each woman would have been required to produce five or six live births in her lifetime just to maintain population levels. Given the perils of childbirth for the mother, this in itself would have been quite a feat.

Although death at what moderns would consider to be an early age would have occurred across the population, a disproportionate number of early deaths fell on the lower rank residents of the villages and the city—a poor person born in Rome in the first century CE had a life expectancy of twenty years! Reasons for this are manifold. Infectious diseases and malnutrition were widespread, and those who made it to age thirty suffered from internal parasites, rotten teeth, poor eyesight, hair lice, and other general maladies. All but the elite were debilitated through protein deficiency. Moreover, poor housing, nonexistent sanitation, and questionable medical care truly made it a culture of the survival of the fittest.

Data about the low life expectancy of men and women can be put together with information about the marriage ages of males and females. It is generally thought that women married young, often in their mid-teens and sometimes as young as eleven years old, although recent research is suggesting that this observation be revised and that women typically were married in their late teens and early twenties. Men were generally about ten years older than women at marriage. Many women could thus outlive their husbands and became widows at an early age, assuming they survived the perils of childbirth. Typically, a man who lost his first wife to illness, injury, or childbirth did not marry a widow, but arranged for a second (or third, or more) marriage, again to a younger girl or woman, with the thought that she would have the strength of youth and the advantage of time to bear him a number of children.

This practice further widened the age gap between man and wife and led to many women becoming widows at very young ages when their older husbands died since very few men lived past their thirties; thus these women became inheritors of their husbands' property. On the other hand, a particularly young and desirable widow could have attracted a second or even a third husband, each of whom could have bequeathed to her his family property. The overall impact of these social practices and Augustan laws was the concentration of a considerable amount of wealth in the hands of young mothers with three or four children, who had the ability to exercise independent economic power and social influence free from the constraints of a *kyrios*.[24]

Bringing all this data back to the book of Acts, we can suggest that from the scant evidence that Luke provides Lydia was involved in financial transactions as a cloth dealer and had oversight of a household. That she was able to offer hospitality to Paul and his colleagues without the approval of anyone suggests that she was not married and was free from the legal constraints of a *kyrios*. The most likely scenario that would apply in her case, and the one that the ancient reader of Luke's document would have most naturally assumed, is that Lydia was perhaps divorced, but more likely widowed, and had given birth to at least three or four children who survived childbirth.

Lydia's Hospitality

In ancient Mediterranean societies ingroup/outgroup dynamics were often at work. That is to say, one often made connections and received help and hospitality from others based on the proximity of the relationship. Relatives were the most proximate and thus were afforded greater hospitality. Other means, however, were available for judging the in-/out-proximity. Long-time neighbors often felt obliged to assist one another. Likewise, should it have been discovered that a visitor to a city hailed from one's home village or town the visitor would have been afforded special invitations to meals. This would also have been the case for persons of like ethnic background.

When we examine Lydia's insistence that Paul and Silas stay in her home (Acts 16:15), we can inquire as to how they have broken into her ingroup. Gender similarities are obviously ruled out, as can be an ethnic connection since Lydia was not from among the *Ioudaioi*. As she was from Thyatira and Paul from Tarsus, a common civic identity was not the connection. They did share a similar social status in that both Lydia and Paul were involved in occupations reviled by the elite and even other artisans and merchants, since both dyeing and leatherwork involved the use of urine at some stage of production. (Since tents were made of leather, when Acts 18:3 notes that Paul was a "tentmaker," it puts him in the wider field of "leatherworker.") Nevertheless, Lydia's newfound belief in Jesus put her squarely in Paul's ingroup, and likewise he in hers. Her invitation is an example of hospitality based on a changed status. We see such changed status hospitality at work elsewhere in the New Testament. When Paul writes to the Corinthians he notes as part of a larger argument that he baptized only a few people:

> I thank God that I baptized none of you except Crispus and Gaius, so that no one can say that you were baptized in my name. (I did baptize also the household of Stephanas; beyond that, I do not know whether I baptized anyone else.) (1 Cor 1:14-16)

It is striking that in a later letter to the Jesus group at Rome, written from Corinth, Paul includes some personal greetings, including, "Gaius, who is host to me and to the whole church, greets you" (Rom 16:23). In Corinth Paul was hosted by one of the persons that he had initially baptized, and this person's house was a primary meeting place for the Jesus group of the city—just like Lydia, who was baptized by Paul and subsequently hosted Paul and a Jesus group. In both cases, Paul broke into the ingroup world of the persons who would become his hosts through his work as a change agent.

Bruce J. Malina and John J. Pilch discuss three stages of hospitality by which a stranger moves from being excluded to being included by the host group, moving from outsider to insider.[25] In stage 1 the stranger is evaluated or tested as to whether he or she fits with the host culture. In the case of Lydia at Philippi, Paul and his companions demonstrate their fluency in Greek (hence they are not *barbaroi*—those who do not even know the language) and their ability to discourse persuasively on socio-religious topics.

In the second stage—the transitional or "liminal" stage—the stranger becomes a guest, including a meal and perhaps even an overnight stay. As such, the stranger becomes part of the household of the host, subject to all the regulations and the honors that belong therein. When Lydia insists that Paul and his companions come to her house (Acts 16:15), she is initiating the second stage. "The word 'prevail' accurately describes the Middle Eastern custom of insistently repeating an offer which the beneficiary is expected to refuse initially but to acquiesce only after a second or third offer."[26]

Paul's later return to Lydia's house after his incarceration (Acts 16:40) reflects the third stage—he is now the transformed stranger. Paul and his companions are known to the host and return as friends to meet and greet those who are part of Lydia's wider social network. Normally, the former stranger would depart a friend, but would carry a debt of gratitude toward the host. In the case of Paul and Lydia, however, Paul has already become Lydia's patron by acting as a change agent and brokering for her a connection with a new, powerful deity.

In terms of the hospitality itself, in an earlier period, particularly among the Greeks, women would have been absent from banqueting. However, by the first century BCE, and in Roman cities, women were seated next to their husbands' couches, and by the first century CE women could recline with their husbands.

> No Roman would hesitate to take his wife to a dinner party, or to allow the mother of his family to occupy the first rooms in his house and to walk about in public. The custom in Greece is completely different: a woman cannot appear at a party unless it is among her relatives; she can only sit in the interior of her house, which is called the women's quarters; this no male can enter unless he is a close relative.[27]

No matter the context, whether "Greek *symposia*, Roman *convivia*, philosophical banquets, sacrificial meals, communal meals of clubs, and Jewish and Christian meals" by the first century all had a common form in which slaves served those who reclined for the meal.[28] This was done in the configuration of a triclinium, three sides for diners set up around a central table. In many houses this configuration was set up in a designated dining room, or perhaps in the garden, by placing three couches around the table. Some houses, and especially the meeting places of workers' associations, had dedicated dining rooms with masonry couches permanently in place. The traditional number of diners was nine—three per couch—although this could have been adapted in order to accommodate more or less participants. In the case of large banquets, multiple triclinia could have been set up in one large room or throughout a number of rooms in the house. In the case of Lydia, we can again extrapolate from the typical to suggest that as their host she would have entertained Paul and his companions in the proper fashion by having her slaves prepare a triclinium and her cook prepare a meal.

The place one reclined on the couch reflected one's public importance since meals were a locus for vying for honor. On the triclinium itself, the bottom of the middle couch was reserved for the guest of honor, with the position to the left occupied by a spouse or companion. On the low couch, a place would have been reserved for the host to the immediate right of the guest of honor. Other places were allocated on the high (H), low (L), and middle (M) couches according to the relative status of the guests—each guest knowing immediately how much honor he was accorded by the host by his position on the couches. All guests reclined on their left elbow while eating from the common table with their right hand. During a meal and especially afterward, diners could shift their posture as comfort dictated, sometimes sitting up or lying back. At Lydia's meal, Paul would have been seated in the place of honor at position M1, with Silas sitting at position M2. Lydia, as host, would have sat at position L7, while the other companions, either her own or those included in the "we" of Acts, would have been distributed appropriately in the remaining places.

The meal served would have been tailored to reflect the honor of the guest, while bringing praise and honor to the host. It would certainly have included leafy vegetables and bread, along

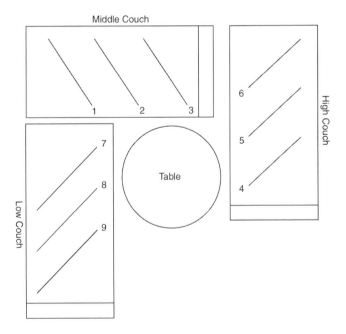

Figure 4. Reclining Positions at a Greco-Roman Banquet

with *garum* (the ubiquitous highly salted fish sauce of the Roman diet), and perhaps fish or meat if Paul was considered a particularly honored guest. The food would have been accompanied by wine, diluted appropriately with water. The cook might have been cautioned against preparing stuffed dormice—a frequent delicacy—since the most common stuffing involved pork. The final course would have involved dried and fresh fruits and perhaps some pastries.[29]

Lydia's Economic Standing

That Lydia was a woman of some financial means is attested in two ways. The first we have already looked at in some detail above—she was the owner of a house and had oversight of her own household, and as such could offer hospitality to Paul and his companions. The second attestation to her economic standing we will discuss in more detail in chapter 4. For now it is sufficient to note that she was a merchant trader who dealt in purple—a *porphyropōlis* in Greek—perhaps buying and selling purple dye in its raw form, or, just as likely, trading in textiles on which purple dye had been used. This indicates the economic means to bulk purchase her wares and/or insure them as they were transported from the east, most likely from the area of Thyatira. It is also suggestive that purple cloth was generally used in clothing for the wealthy. Although there was an imitation purple dye that was used in material for the lower ranks, who liked to imitate the elite, purple still represented a luxury item and as such demanded the clientele of the wealthy. We find a possible analogy to Lydia in an inscription from the late Republic that indicates that a woman, Veturia, was engaged in the purple trade, possibly without her husband, and was quite wealthy.[30]

Although some have argued that Lydia was poor, each aspect of Lydia's profile—purple dealing, autonomy, heading a household, showing hospitality, and traveling—"decreases the probability of her being very poor" and when put together "suggest an income above subsistence."[31] Peter Oakes goes so far as to speculate on the composition of her household, suggesting "maybe three or four Asian relatives and half-a-dozen slaves, either domestic or engaged in her work."[32] While I would not be willing to go so far as to posit the number or types of her domestic companions, I do agree with Oakes that she had access to an income that put her into the segment of society described for Philippi in chapter 1 above as the "service groups."

There are several ways in which Lydia may have acquired her economic fluidity, although a few in particular stand out as possibilities. If she had been a slave she may have gained her money through the financial responsibility given to her during her period of servitude. Slaves were often allowed to keep some of the profit they made, thus giving them an incentive to work hard. Additionally, many slaves were granted substantial bequests along with manumission at the death of their master. As many freed slaves maintained a close relationship with former masters they often received a legacy when the master died.

A second means by which Lydia may have gained her economic freedom is through inheritance of money from her father's estate. Liberal laws in the Augustan and Claudian periods led to more freedom for women to inherit from their fathers and to bequeath to whomever they wanted, the latter leading to women bequeathing their own estates to daughters, sisters, or other women of choice. A third possible means by which money may have come her way is through her husband, either in a divorce settlement, although this is unlikely as it was rare, or through inheritance of her deceased husband's estate.

Given Lydia's ability to act of her own accord without a *kyrios*, it seems to me that any of these three scenarios are possible. First, as a freedwoman it would have been necessary for her to have four or more children survive infancy. Second, as the inheritor of a portion of her father's estate she would have needed to be in a *sine manu* marriage relationship, wherein she or her family maintained control over her goods. Or third, as a widow or divorcée, she also would have needed to be in a *sine manu* marriage. In both of the latter cases at least three of her children would have had to survive infancy. Any combination of these or other possibilities could also have led to a woman such as Lydia gaining economic freedom.

Lydia's Patronage

Paul's experiences in Macedonia were full of suffering and affliction (1 Thess 2:2; 2 Cor 7:5). Nevertheless, his comments on the Jesus groups of Macedonia reflect positively on them. They contributed generously to his collection of relief funds for the Jesus group in Jerusalem even when they were suffering persecution and were in poverty (Rom 15:26-27; 2 Cor 8:1-5; cf. 1 Thess 1:7-8). The Macedonians provided monetary support to Paul while he was living in Corinth (2 Cor 11:9), although it is likely that this refers to the support given by the Jesus group at Philippi, as this group was the only one that supported Paul in his work outside Macedonia (Phil 4:14-17). The Philippian group also sent an important and popular man to Paul to assist him in his ministry (Phil 2:25-30). The Philippian Jesus group was vigorous in its financial support for Paul in his travels in Macedonia and in Achaia. Some of its group members probably enjoyed at least a moderate level of income. Very likely some of them were like Lydia, located among the merchants who had migrated to the area from Asia Minor.

The women of Macedonia had a reputation and tradition of initiative and influence. This trait was borne out among the believers noted in the Philippian Jesus group, where women did have a leadership role, as is suggested by the mention by name of two prominent women there, Euodia and Syntyche, and the dispute they were having (Phil 4:2). The rhetoric of Paul's letter clearly indicates these women were influential and thus occupied positions of leadership in the group. That a woman, Lydia, provided Paul with local support fits with a wider pattern of Paul receiving financial support from women. Phoebe in Cenchreae was a patron to Paul and probably had a large house (Rom 16:1-2). According to Luke, "leading women" of Thessalonica were among the early Jesus devotees (Acts 17:4), and in Beroea "Greek women . . . of high standing" joined (Acts 17:12).

By having Lydia invite Paul and his companions to her house, and by having her host a gathering of the "brothers and sisters," Luke is presenting Lydia as a patron of the seminal Jesus group at Philippi. Like many women of her time, she sought to use her economic fluidity to create opportunities to enhance her status, the primary means by which to do so being patronage. By hosting Paul and his companions Lydia stood to become Paul's patron if and when he remained in the city. The relationship was, however, more complex, since Paul first brokered for Lydia an even greater divine benefactor than that which she had previously. Thus, Lydia became Paul's client. Her hospitality did not make her Paul's patron but rather was an act of reciprocity for the benefits she had gained through Paul. In the culture of the time, there was no appreciable difference between material and immaterial benefits. Further, Paul's willingness to accept her hospitality fit into his role as a change agent, in which he was required to solidify and stabilize the change that had taken place, a task made easier if he spent time continuing to teach Lydia and her household, as is inferred in Acts 16:16, which notes that on *another* day Paul and his companions were returning to the place of prayer.

The accumulation of wealth without social payoffs was considered of little value in the first-century Mediterranean world. Well-to-do persons had two main avenues open to them for the sought-after social payoffs: benefaction and patronage. Benefaction was an outright donation of some goods or service of value to the whole community. There was no further reciprocity expected aside from the public acknowledgment of the donor's public spiritedness that entailed a great grant of honor. Patronage on the other hand was a reciprocal relationship in which a well-placed person provided favors to one asking for or requiring something that the client needed. The client, in turn was required to give continued grants of honor to the patron by acknowledging the patron's favor to others, defending the patron before detractors or offering assistance as required by the patron. A favor (Greek: *charis*; Latin: *gratia*) was something a client needed because she or he did not have it or did not have it available at a given time.

Patterns of patronage extended beyond individuals to include favors bestowed on elective social formations, or what are often called "voluntary associations" or "guilds." These groups, which we will explore in a bit more detail in chapter 4, were comprised of men or women who met together on the basis of shared interests such as a common occupation or the enacting of rituals for a particular deity. Inscriptional evidence shows that women acted as patrons to such social formations by funding their banquets and festivals, providing investments for them as sources of income, or donating meeting places for them in the form of property and/or a building. Many such groups regularly met in a house, sometimes even the house of their patron. In exchange for such favors, the patron expected public honors commensurate with the level of the gift—the greater the gift, the more public the praise and willingness to reciprocate.

If we imagine Lydia as a woman with the means and interest in patronage then it is unlikely that the favor she bestowed on Paul and the early Jesus group was her first such social contract. At the same time, unless Lydia herself was among the elite of the city, which is quite unlikely, she too would have been the client of others and she, in turn, would have needed to approach her patrons, on whom she would have depended for business contracts, business loans, and new contacts. Such was the way of business in the Roman world. A business owner spent much of her time negotiating social contracts in a way that ensured the continuation of work for her slaves and employees. During Paul's time in prison, such networks likely proved important for the spread of the message of Jesus—his resurrection of the dead and his inauguration of an alternative government, a "kingdom of God." Having discovered this promise of protection and a better afterlife, Lydia would naturally have wanted to display to others her great fortune. Any wise clients would have quickly wanted to acknowledge that Lydia's god was also good for them, and thus would have wanted to become involved in the *pietas* that it entailed—if only in outward appearance. Thus, it is not surprising that on their release from prison, Paul and Silas return to Lydia's house and find there a gathering of "brothers and sisters" (*adelphoi*).

In recording the story Luke can assume that Lydia's newfound belief has spread not only within her household but also among her network of clients, and thus Luke can label them as *adelphoi*, a fictive-kinship term used among Jesus believers as well as among other groups of like-minded persons. Once Paul left Philippi, we can surmise that faith in Jesus continued to spread, albeit slowly and in limited circles, through the overlapping networks of patrons and clients, businesspeople and customers, that radiated out from and around Lydia (see fig. 5). As Oakes notes, "Lydia and her household would also have represented a range of other social points of entry into the Philippian population: in her own case, among Asian migrant traders of reasonable wealth."[33] By the time Paul writes to the Jesus group in Philippi some time later, he assumes a wider group than simply that based in the single household of Lydia.[34]

The ability of women in the imperial period to find some freedom from the domestic sphere and enter into public life was possible in large part due to the Romanization that was occurring in the Augustan and post-Augustan periods. There is a wide-ranging debate about the use of the word "Romanization," although it has become the standard scholarly means to talk about the process of Roman cultural values spreading from Rome into Italy and then to the western and eastern parts of the Roman Empire.[35] The processes and outcomes were by no means uniform as they were affected by many factors, including pre-existing cultural elements, local elite practices, and social competition. That Roman culture was so indebted to Greek culture

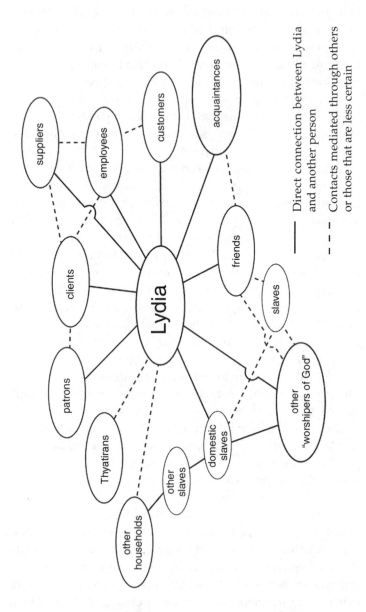

Figure 5. A Selection of Potential Contacts in Lydia's Network

over the previous two centuries meant that there was not a complete disjuncture between Roman and Greek values, making the Augustan values easily adopted and adapted in the eastern parts of the empire—the new values were often couched in the clothing of the traditional values. The overall effect was a "cultural bricolage" in which preexisting cultural elements took on new functions and meanings in the new context of Roman rule. All members of a society undergoing Romanization were involved in negotiating the new functions and meanings, including the nonelite members.

Romanization of the Greek East opened up venues for some women to participate more fully in public life, taking up occupations and fulfilling roles such as benefactor to the city or to one or more groups within the city in full view of their contemporaries, as attested in public monuments and inscriptions. We will look in more detail at the context of Lydia's occupation in chapter 4, but first we must turn our attention to the ancient woman's first point of entry from the domestic sphere into the public view—the marketplace.

CHAPTER 3

Lydia in the Marketplace

L ife in a Greco-Roman city was very structured—a place for everyone and everyone in his or her place! This hierarchical view of society was held commonly throughout the empire. Daily relations involved the careful maintenance of social boundaries, social relations, and the agonistic jockeying for the limited supply of honor distributed among one's peers. The marketplace was not simply a place to purchase goods; it was the social location for exchanging gossip, greeting friends, negotiating business contracts, and, above all, participating in the back and forth tussle for recognition of honor. One's neighbors were knowledgeable about much of what was happening in one's life—and if they weren't, they made it their business to become so informed. Each person was aware that any outing into the public was an occasion to display one's status through clothing, position at banquets, seat in the theater, and so on, and thus remind others of one's place in the hierarchy of society. Although women's roles within the public sphere and its competition for honor were limited, changes introduced by Augustus concerning marriage and children (see chap. 2) had the ancillary, and largely unintended, effect of creating new opportunities for women to participate in public life.

Rank and Honor

The social hierarchy itself, the *ordo*, was clear to all and was structured so as to ensure that those at the very top remained in a minority, albeit a financially and politically powerful minority.[1] At the pinnacle of the social hierarchy were the emperor and his extended family. Although having little or no legal status themselves due to their status as slaves or freed persons, the numerically large *familia Caesaris* ("Caesar's household") wielded great economic and social power throughout the empire in the name of the emperor. A large group of the *familia Caesaris* was housed with the imperial household and employed in domestic service to the emperor's family and managed imperial establishments and estates. Another large group was employed in a wide range of administrative posts in the civil service spread throughout the empire. Most likely members of the *familia Caesaris* resided in Philippi. When writing to the Philippians, Paul includes greetings from "those of the emperor's household" (Phil 4:22), suggesting that some of the thousands who carried this status had come to believe in Jesus and were at least familiar to the Philippian believers.

Directly below the emperor in the social hierarchy was the senatorial rank, the most prestigious of all ranks as membership was limited to several hundred families deemed worthy on the basis of birth, wealth, and moral excellence. Since a senator was required under Augustus to purchase his seat in the senate for a substantial sum of money, the established patrician hold on the rank was starting to slip with the rise of "new money" upstarts who did not carry the ancient pedigrees. Nevertheless, overall membership of the senatorial rank was closely guarded and there was little opportunity for mobility into it, as most senators encouraged their sons to follow their career path into the senate.

The aristocratic equestrian rank required high birth, wealth, and moral excellence, but at a lower level than that required of senators. As a result, it was a larger rank and likely numbered in the thousands, although still limited for the newly wealthy by the requirement that one be the son of a free man. The most privileged among the equestrians lived in Rome, with occasional forays in foreign postings as political expediency required, while the majority were local elite in Roman provinces. The decurion rank was that of a councilor and it was the place where the ambitious could begin their family's generational ascent into the senatorial rank. The definition of "respectable birth" for decurion status required at the very least having a freedman as a father. Decurions held civil service jobs throughout the empire and were required to contribute generously to the public treasury when entering into office. Although this was expensive, the right administrative post could allow the ambitious decurion to gain back much more in the form of taxes, fees, bribes, and kickbacks.

The emperor's family, senators, equestrians, and decurions formed the elite of the social hierarchy, although even together they were still a tiny fraction of the population. There was then a vast gulf between the elite and the rest of the population, as there was no middle class in the sense of an intermediate group with independent economic resources or social standing. Instead, there was a mass of the humble free and below them the slaves and outcasts. Nevertheless, even the great mass of nonelites had their own ranking that affected their legal and social position in society, and some free and freed persons attained significant wealth, albeit limited in its purchasing power since they were still barred from rising too high in the elite ranks. Within the ranks of free and freeborn relative status was determined by factors such as family background and occupation, among other things. Roman citizenship was available to freeborn and freed and provided legal protection against particularly gruesome forms of interrogation and execution to which the noncitizen was liable.

Those who had been born into freedom, whose parents were either free or freed, were ranked higher in the social estimation than those who at some point in their past had been enslaved. Wealth had little bearing on this, and many freed persons had accumulated wealth beyond that of free persons.[2] Nevertheless, they still bore the stigma of their former servile status. Slaves had the legal status of property, a "speaking tool" (*instrumentum vocale*), rather than personhood, and could be bought and sold, pampered or abused at the will of their master. Although slaves could cohabit with one another, they were considered kinless and there was no legal protection against a master breaking up a slave's family among different buyers. Nevertheless, under a good master a slave's life could be vastly better than the lot of the urban poor, since a slave could rely on security, food, and shelter. Yet even among slaves there was social stratification, with a higher ranking for domestic slaves and those running commercial enterprises for their masters than for those forced to undertake manual labor.

Rank could be indicated in a number of ways in the public sphere. Senators and their sons wore a toga with a broad purple stripe; equestrians wore gold rings and a narrow purple stripe; upper ranks had better seats in the theater and larger quantity and better quality of food at public banquets and distributions (the poor were not given more food but less, as an indicator of their lower status). A person of lower rank did not approach a person of higher rank as an equal but rather as a beneficiary. Such stratification governed all social interactions, day in and day out. Behind all of it was the estimation of a person's honor, since ultimately one's status was tied to one's honor. The higher one's rank the more honor one was accorded, and honor, more than wealth, formed the backbone of the social economy in antiquity—it was a core value that saturated every aspect of life.

Honor was a community-based value that depended on public recognition—a person's worth was grounded in what others thought of that person. It was through this community sanctioned honor that one recognized social superiors, equals, and inferiors. Its opposite, dishonor, was the public denial of a person's claim. Through the public validation of a person's claim to worthiness that person internalized his own self-worth. This runs counter to the predominant individualistic concern for self-worth in North America today. Whereas we might be able to claim "I'm okay and you're okay," in antiquity that would not be acceptable! A person's sense of being "okay" depended on his ability to maintain honor, and the very presence of another person presented a threat to his honor, as he might lose honor in the eyes of those around him.

Honor was recognized under two general categories. The first was ascribed honor, which was inherited through family or communities or persons of power. A man's name served as his credit rating and a guarantee of trustworthiness. This is the reason genealogies were so important in antiquity. The second category, acquired honor, was gained by excelling over others through a system of challenge and response. Every social inter-action was an opportunity for a man to display his honor— through his dress, his gestures, his place at a meal, his witty dinner repartee, his ability to throw extravagant parties, the food he served, the house he lived in, the number of clients he bene-facted; the list is endless as every occasion was governed by the implicit, embedded rules governing honor. Ultimately, ascribed honor was of more consequence than acquired honor, and a man's family name and rank in the Roman *ordo* took precedence over his ability to display his wealth. Thus self-made, rich mer-chants were considered to possess less honor than a poor man from an important family. This is quite different from North America where the "little guy who makes it big" is a key part of the American Dream. Failure to maintain one's honor resulted in a man being shamed—an indication of a public lack of honor. Very often the only mechanism to remove a deep-seated or po-tentially long-lasting condition of being shamed was to do the "honorable" thing and commit suicide.

To this point I have deliberately been using gender-exclusive language, since honor-shame societies are highly gendered. In such a culture, women had shame, but in a positive sense insofar as they understood their role in maintaining the honor of their family. They were sensitive to social status and roles and did not transgress them. Persons such as prostitutes (and actors!) were considered shameless because they did not possess sensitivity to their proper place. They did not respect the boundaries or norms of the honor system. Honor competitions were played out primarily among males. Tragically, females were often reduced to the status of pawns in the competition for honor. For example, rape was viewed as the invasion of a husband's or father's honor, which was a more serious infraction, in his mind, than the traumatic effect on his wife or daughter.

In antiquity honor, like wealth, was considered a limited good. For modern persons (at least those in the so-called first world) goods are, in principle, unlimited. If there is a shortage we can either produce more or redistribute from where there is a surplus. If someone gains more, we do not assume it has been taken from someone else. In antiquity, wealth was a limited quantity. For a person to gain more wealth, that person had to take it away from someone else. All goods, it was thought, existed in a limited, finite supply that was already distributed. This extended beyond material goods to include honor, friendship, love, power, security, and status. If someone had a larger piece of the pie, someone else had a smaller piece. The pie never grew larger (that is, there was no expanding economy). In order to gain honor one had to take it away from another person. Wealthy persons expended fortunes trying to gain honor from among their peers.

Those who did succeed in accumulating honor were wary of the envious, as the latter bore the evil eye, which could cause loss of honor, loss of property, injury, or even death. Out-group persons along with certain animals, demons, and deities were thought to possess the evil eye inherently. In others, envy worked in the heart but manifested itself in the evil eye, since ancients understood the heart and eyes as linked. If one caught the evil eye—that is, made contact with a possessor of such—then all sorts of evil could occur. Thus, special amulets and incantations were employed to ward off the evil eye.[3] (Even today the evil eye is warded off with special amulets in some circum-Mediterranean countries.)

A society in which there is constant competition to gain honor at the expense of others is called an agonistic society. There is a constant jockeying for public recognition of one's own relative worth—namely, relative to others in that same context. Such jockeying took place through direct conflicts such as athletic abilities, verbal arguments, and courtroom debates, but also manifested itself in benefactions, hospitality, banquets, clothing, indeed in all aspects of ancient Mediterranean life. Wealth existed only for gaining honor; it was not saved for the future but invested whenever possible in public display. Plutarch observes, "Most people think themselves deprived of wealth if they are prevented from showing off; the display is made in the superfluities, not the essentials of life" (*Cato the Elder*, 18).[4] Interactions of challenge and riposte took place among those considered to have an equal amount of honor. In a modern culture we might phrase it "pick on someone your own size." There was little gain in challenging a weaker person, and much could be lost. How a man faired in an agonistic encounter was judged by observers and his honor rose or fell with his performance.

Although honor was an important value, what was honorable could vary from region to region or village to village; it was considerably different among elite and nonelite portions of the population. Peasants associated honor with self-sufficiency— being able to provide a subsistence living for one's family without recourse to others to meet basic needs; accumulation of surplus was shameful thievery.[5] Urban elites associated honor with having large numbers of friends upon whom one could rely for favors and with accumulating sufficient surplus to be able to dole out favors in a display of wealth. Both the elite and nonelite understood the importance of honor, but each had its own perception of how honor should be obtained or preserved.

Honor and shame were not static qualities even within a given locale—they were highly contextualized. What constituted an honorable man in one context might change in a different context. While a more general view of honor in society might require careful negotiation of behavior, a smaller group context would allow for the relaxation of some social regulations governing that behavior. For example, women were generally not seen in, and were discouraged from, political leadership roles. Even in public their roles were that of shame in the positive sense—knowing the cultural boundaries and not crossing them (perhaps better called "modesty"). Nevertheless, in a different setting, a woman could take on leadership roles around organizing and regulating group behavior. Hence, we find public temples in which priest-esses were clearly in top leadership positions. Likewise in elective social formations we find women in leadership. Thus, when Lydia became the host and leader of a newly formed Jesus group in her house, she was still within the acceptable boundaries of honor and shame in that culture. This was not transgressive be-havior, for reasons we shall examine in the next section.

Women in Public

Since the primary social institution was kinship, and gender roles were focal in kinship institutions, Greek social values tended toward the conservative when it came to public roles for women. Women were expected to remain in the domestic sphere quite separate from the world of men. Roman men likewise upheld traditional virtues for Roman women, in particular *pietas*, which encompassed a sense of duty, devotion to family, respect, and loyalty to traditional religion. *Fides* described a woman's faithfulness to a single man (a virtue not often reciprocated) even beyond his death, while *pudicitia* similarly emphasized proper sexual conduct.[6] Despite this conservatism, by the first century Roman women were appearing more frequently in public. Ac-cording to a first-century BCE writer, Cornelius Nepos, Greek women sat secluded in the interior of the house. In contrast, he says, Roman women accompanied their husbands to dinner parties.[7] Roman women also visited the public baths, which most often had separate sections for men and women, or separate times for each gender. By the end of the reign of Augustus women from all ranks of society were taking an active part in the public, social, and commercial life of the city, in large part due to Augustus' attempts to uphold family values.

As we noted above, Augustus introduced laws that were meant to reward elite men who did their duty for the empire by siring as many children as possible.[8] Those who failed to do so were passed over when it came to civil service jobs or career advancements. Those whose families continued to grow could expect to see their careers advance quickly from job to better job. As part of the marriage reforms, Augustus addressed the concern of fathers that, should they marry off their daughters, they stood to lose not only the dowry but any other property they might give or bequeath to their daughter, especially since the daughter's husband had the right to terminate the marriage but the daughter did not. The new Augustan laws allayed these fears by granting to the *paterfamilias* the right to protect his property through *sine manu* marriage, among other things. No longer was it a threat to one's estate to allow a daughter to be married. In addressing the reluctance of women to undergo the painful and often terminal process of childbirth, the introduction of the *ius (trium) liberorum* held out hope for those women who gave birth to three or four (or more) children.

Other legislation aimed at public morality among the elite linked the status of a woman to that of her husband—a woman was judged according to the honor of her husband, and thus it behooved her to do all in her power to promote her husband's honor. As a consequence, however, women began to use their own property to participate in the very thing that society dictated brought honor to a household, namely, public displays of status and wealth. Although Augustus had not necessarily intended to do so, he had provided women with a means and a right to more liberty than they had experienced before, or ever would again for a long period after the retraction of their freedoms in the second century. Elite women began to offer their patronage to local organizations of a social, commercial, religious, or even political nature. In doing so, these elite women forged for themselves public status and recognition, often carrying it on long after their husbands died. In this new configuration, "Roman women had access to money and power, and their fortunes were linked to those of the state. As men prospered, so did women."[9] The existence of these new venues that opened for women helps explain why women such as Mary Magdalene (Luke 8:1-3), Phoebe (Rom 16:1-2), or Chloe (1 Cor 1:11) were able to provide financial support for Jesus and the groups that formed in his name.

There was more, however. Having had a taste of the freedoms enjoyed for so long by men, these women pursued their full flavor. According to the contemporary moralists of the time (namely, elite men!) writing in factual documents as well as fictional tales such as novels, these "new" women began to neglect their domestic duties in order to pursue a public role. They became full participants at banquets and reclined with male guests, they attended the theaters where they enjoyed seating near the front (places normally reserved for men), and they began to ensure that their dress was such that it did not draw attention to their modesty and decorum but, like men, drew attention to their privileged status and their wealth. More shockingly (again, for the elite men), these new women were exercising freedom and pleasure in sexual activity outside of the relationships with their husbands, indulging in it for pleasure rather than for procreation.

The Augustan reforms had their initial impact in these ways for elite women at Rome, but the impact soon began to spread throughout the empire. The new ethos became known in a number of ways, including the depiction of elite women in portraiture and on coins, through the imperial deployment of government officials and their wives in urban centers to the west and east of Rome, and through explicit attempts to bring Roman values to all the inhabitants. Despite a relatively small bureaucratic system (compared to the size of the empire), there was not a cultural isolationism in the East, especially in colonies such as Philippi or Corinth. "Rome skillfully engaged in the transformation of values by highly sophisticated forms of propaganda and so succeeded that non-Romans embraced Roman values as part of first-century modernity," even at the provincial level.[10] With this penetration of values came the depiction not only of the traditional picture of women and their roles; it also brought to attention the "new" women and their values and actions.

As is often the case in social interaction, the elites, the wellborn wealthy and the well-known, were looked upon as trendsetters, leading the way in new fashion and presenting the general public with acceptable actions that served as the norm. We see this even today in the West (and beyond), where the wealthy and well-known (even if not well-born) public entertainers (Hollywood stars and professional athletes) are noted for "who" (not what) they are wearing at large, public galas. These individualistic stars, like their collectivistic predecessors in the royal families of Europe, have the wealth to allow them to purchase the biggest and the best of all the good things in life. In so doing, they signal what all the rest of us should and could have, if only we could rise to the top, like them. Advertisers, however, know well how to reverse this psychology, using these same stars to convince audiences that if we purchase the same things as the stars (or less expensive copies) we will "be" like them. So it was in the Roman Empire. Elite men and women, especially those of the imperial household, provided the general public with trendsetting lifestyles. Thus, when the emperor Hadrian first sported a beard in the early-second century, he set off a wave of facial hair growth not seen on men since the days of Greek ascendancy.

Across the empire, the fashion styles and trends of the imperial elite were broadcast by way of coins, statues, and paintings.[11] Their portraiture was used to depict how, in the eyes of elite males, women should dress and act appropriately. Scenes of *decorum* and *pietas* come to dominate in such conservative depictions. In contrast, however, women noticed that the imperial women went about unveiled in some portraiture and on their streets when they were in town. The imperial women were heralded in inscriptions for the great benefactions that they gave to cities and organizations. And the racy stories about their scandalous sexual escapades were the subject of local gossip in the marketplace. Stories of up-and-coming women working alongside their husbands circulated with the economic and social freedoms trickling down to those below the elite in Rome. Although elite women living outside Rome may not have had the means or the will to act with the full confidence of the imperial women who are attested in the literature and on inscriptions, they would have had in such women models of the respectability of public display and benefaction in the Augustan period. As Juvenal notes, "What woman will not follow when an empress leads the way?" (*Satires*, 6.617).[12] As new marriage laws began impacting women who were freeborn or freed, they too began imitating their "betters" in matters of public benefaction, extra-domestic employment, and less conservative sexual mores. In provincial towns women participated more regularly in the public sphere and in the workplace, but those who took advantage of the latitude in freedom were more likely from the upper or up-and-coming ranks of society.

The consequences of Augustan legislation for the rise of the "new" woman in Rome and the deployment of that image across the empire, including the East, as part of the intended and unintended Romanization of occupied peoples created conditions of relative freedoms for many women. Living in one of the most Romanized of all the urban centers outside of the capital, Lydia would have been exposed to and influenced by these new opportunities for women. We noted above her ability to own her own house and make her own decisions about providing hospitality to foreign men. There is another passing note in Luke's narrative that is likewise linked to the social conditions of the time—Lydia's ability to engage in public in the workforce as a merchant in the purple trade. It is to this aspect that we will turn our attention in the next chapter.

CHAPTER 4

Lydia in the Workplace

As the Roman Empire expanded, trade across all parts of the empire and beyond prospered. Shipping routes provided access throughout the Mediterranean Sea, while the estimated fifty-three thousand miles of Roman roads stretched from Britannia in the West to Syria and beyond in the East, as far as the areas of modern-day India and China. The primary purpose of the roads was the swift and unhindered movement of military legions from one trouble spot to another, although even the threat of such a quick response to an uprising served to maintain the *pax Romana* in all but the frontier locales. The presence of the Roman military had an impact on local road conditions. When not on patrol or engaged in police actions, Roman soldiers were employed in building and repairing the vast network of roads and bridges. Their engineering ability is attested by the endurance of the road system, much of which remains intact today, and small parts of which are still in use. The military presence on the roads and at sea also served to suppress much of the banditry and piracy that had plagued earlier times. Epictetus notes that "Caesar has obtained for us a profound peace. There are neither wars nor battles, nor great robberies nor piracies, but we may travel at all hours, and sail from east to west."[1]

Under these peaceful conditions—purchased at the hefty price of iron rule and heavy taxation of colonized peoples—commercial trade flourished as did the movement of itinerant philosophers and proponents of new religious movements. There were four principal trade routes in the Roman Empire, two primarily by sea and two primarily by land. One of the two land routes involved the Appian Way from Rome to Brundisium, a crossing of the Adriatic Sea by ship to Dyrrachium, and then the Egnatian Way across Macedonia and into Asia at the Bosporus. Along the route in Macedonia there were major sea ports at Thessalonica and at Neapolis, the latter serving the colony of Philippi. It is conceivable that Lydia was among the many merchants in the city who imported goods from Asia Minor, since Philippi was an accessible and frequent trade stop for goods by sea or overland.

Women at Work

In antiquity an artisan's life was not easy. For the most part artisans could earn their daily bread, if they worked long and hard enough (cf. 1 Thess 4:11-12). Some could even rise to modest affluence and thus have money to spend. Most people, however, could expect to earn enough daily to purchase bread and perhaps some smoked fish and thus feed their families, but savings were out of the question.[2] Artisans were considered lower rank by the elite; their work was considered that of a slave, even if the artists themselves were freeborn. Artisans were "stigmatized as slavish, uneducated, and often useless" and "were frequently reviled or abused, often victimized, seldom if ever invited to dinner, and never accorded status."[3] Bending over to work was also considered a slavish position that no self-respecting elite person would willingly assume. A free man who took up a trade was viewed as having done something humiliating. Plying a trade was denigrated by the elite since it left no time for building friendships or developing one's virtue. Thus, artisans were considered incapable of attaining virtue or else they were viewed as uneducated.

Small-scale traders were not viewed much better, since they too were involved in slavish work and proved an irritant for the elite, as seen in a scene from Plautus' comedic play in which a retinue of tradespersons come to his atrium to collect their payment, including "the clothes dyer, . . . sellers of purple dye, sellers of yellow dye, and fabric strainers . . . all cluttering up your atrium." And when they are paid, "into your atrium come more dyers . . . and any other wretched gallows-bird who wants some money" (*Aulularia* [*The Concealed Treasure*], 505–22).[4] In contrast, large-scale merchants were accepted by some as contributing to society, as the words from Cicero suggest:

> Trade, if it is on a small scale, is to be considered vulgar, but if wholesale and on a large scale, importing large quantities from all parts of the world and distributing to many without misrepresentation, it is not to be greatly disparaged. Nay, it even seems to deserve the lightest respect, if those who are engaged in it, satiated, or rather, I should say, satisfied with the fortunes they have made, make their way from the port to a country estate, as they have often made it from the sea to port. (*On Duty*, 1.42, LCL)

Given Cicero's own background as an equestrian whose fortunes in trade led to his political elevation to the senatorial class, we should perhaps be wary that his words are meant more for legitimating his own status. Since Cicero had friends and family among the large-scale traders, he did not disparage them, but did disparage those below. Cicero's contemporaries, however, are known to have looked down upon the likes of Cicero as "new money"—whatever the size of their trading operations.

For those of established families in the senatorial rank, the blue bloods, the likes of Cicero were seen as interlopers. These elite attitudes trickled down to the lower ranks of the social order, but were adjusted accordingly. Smaller operations would have vied with one another for positions of honor, and would of necessity have looked down upon those who were not traders, but who worked with their hands. These artisans, in turn, had their own ranking, placing one type of occupation below another in the hierarchy.

We noted earlier the importance of ingroup/outgroup distinctions for households and extended families. This ancient Mediterranean value also had an impact on how small businesses were structured and organized. There were very few large-scale businesses; most were family-run operations, with the head of the household overseeing operations and family members involved in the labor side and, as much as it existed, management. This latter category was largely made up of direct family members, particularly sons, or, more often, slaves. Lydia was not likely from one of the larger trading operations that Cicero describes. Luke's description limits her to one particular type of import goods at best, either dye or dyed cloth. Nevertheless, as a merchant rather than a manufacturer she would have had some relative status in the mercantile rank.

Generally, in the Greco-Roman world, as with most ancient societies, women worked in the domestic sphere, either maintaining a household or, in some instances, working in occupations ancillary to the household such as childcare (midwives, wet nurses, nannies), food preparation (markets, bread and beer making, eateries), and textile production (spinning, weaving, dyeing, making clothes). Some women who were "particularly enterprising were able to turn their domestic-based activities into lucrative occupations."[5] Women were highly valued in such occupations, largely since they had developed their skills for generations, often in unpaid labor within the household. Whether or not women worked in these occupations they were associated with particular social values. For example, spinning and weaving became such powerful symbols that goddesses and elite women were depicted in literature and in visual media as undertaking such tasks. "These ancient media images of women working at their spindles or looms promoted the cultural ideals of elite women's industriousness and proper fulfillment of their matronly roles"[6]—as is perfunctorily expressed in the tomb epigram of the archetypal Roman matron Claudia: "She kept house, she made wool" (*CIL* 2.1211, cited in full in chap. 2). In reality, slaves and freed persons, the bottom of the Roman *ordo*, were typically those involved in textile production, so conservative Roman values that linked women to textile work really served to denigrate women even as they sought to offer praise.

By Augustan times, however, a number of women had broken free of the production side of commercial businesses and ran their own factories or shops as managers or owners, sometimes alongside their husbands, sometimes alone. Representations of women at work in the imperial period show them in occupations of sales or service of products including clothing, food, meat, fish, and luxury items such as perfumes or dye. Among the paintings from a shop in Pompeii one notes the predominance of representations of males and females at work with textiles, including that of a shop owner with a piece of cloth in hand and a woman, probably his wife, behind a counter making a sale to a seated customer. Clarke points out that:

> No elite person would commission such a representation of him- or herself. Yet among the working non-elites—from slaves to freedpersons to the freeborn—self-representations surrounded by images of one's trade or profession are common. . . . This visual representation demonstrated that for non-elites there was no stigma attached to work, but rather that—under the protection of the gods and in full view of all—work was to be celebrated.[7]

Some women attained even greater honor, as in the case of a wealthy woman named Eumachia, who lived in Pompeii sometime before the eruption of Mount Vesuvius in 79 CE. She makes an interesting study with which to compare Lydia, as Eumachia had connections with wool dyers (fullers) and carried on her own business dealings. An inscription on the largest business building on the forum reads:

> Eumachia, daughter of Lucius, public priestess, in her own
> name and that of her son, Marcus Numistrius Fronto, built
> at her own expense the outside porch, the cryptoporticus,
> and the porticoes and dedicated them to Concordia Au-
> gusta and Pietas.[8]

Although her family made bricks, Eumachia was a patron of the
fullers association in the city. In recognition of her benefaction,
the fullers erected a statue of her inside the building. Lydia was
not likely a merchant on the scale of Eumachia. What Eumachia
and countless others demonstrate, however, is the involvement
of women in occupations outside of the home during the first
century CE.

During the Roman imperial period clothing was in high demand and expensive. The high demand resulted in a number of
people being employed in the clothing industry, including weavers, spinners, fullers, and dyers. In a comprehensive study of
inscriptions, Susan Treggiari lists a number of women employed
in the urban staff of upper-rank slave owners in the period from
Augustus to the early-second century. Many of the jobs for
women involved clothes: clothes-folders, spinners, weavers,
managers of entire operations of wool working—including the
distribution of wool, spinning, and the finishing of a garment—
tailors/clothes-makers, and clothes menders. Treggiari concludes that while women were absent from outdoor work in
town and from administrative jobs, they predominated as personal attendants to women, midwives, nurses, and entertainers.[9]
In clothes production they outnumbered men about three to one.
It is also important to note that women often shared in the profession of their husbands and could carry on the profession of
the husband should there be no son to take over the business.
In sum, Lydia's position as a purple dealer is not unusual. Even
as a woman, Luke's notation of her occupation would not have
given his readers pause. So, it is to the nature of her occupation
that we will next turn our attention.

Dealing Purple

The manufacture and trade of purple dye and purple goods was a well-organized and important industry during the Roman Empire, and it is within this scope of occupations that Acts 16:14 locates Lydia by noting that she was a "purple dealer" (*porphyropōlis*).[10] The trade of purple dye became an imperial monopoly, controlled by the various emperors over time, perhaps from as early as the time of Claudius. If Lydia dealt in true purple she would have been under imperial control and may even have been a member of "the emperor's household" (Phil 4:22). The slaves and freed persons that belonged to the imperial household were probably the most mobile group in Roman society, and thus it would have been no surprise to find one of them in Philippi. Against this suggestion, however, is the existence of the manufacture of cheaper quality (non-imperial) purple in Thyatira and the use of the name Lydia for freeborn women outside of Lydia (as opposed to it being a slave name meaning "the Lydian"). Thus, a direct connection cannot be assumed between Lydia of Acts and the household of Caesar.[11]

There were a number of methods used to obtain purple dye in antiquity. Along the Syrian and Phoenician coast is found a mollusk called the Tyrian *murex* that contains a small bladder that holds a tiny amount of juice. In antiquity this juice was extracted, purified, and manufactured into varying grades of purple dye. Dye from seashells was manufactured in a few places, but the best dye was thought to come from Tyre in Syria. Purple extracted from *murex* was very expensive, even in the second century CE when its popularity was at a peak. Often cloth was double-dyed in order to give it more consistency, although this served to increase the price (Pliny the Elder, *Natural History*, 9.125-34).

Two other methods of manufacturing dye were less expensive but actually gave more of a red than purple dye. One method involved the roots of the madder plant (*rubia*). This type of dye was manufactured in Western Anatolia, including the city of Thyatira, Lydia's hometown. In literary and epigraphic writings

Thyatira is often linked to purple production, with Homer placing purple dyeing very early in the areas of Lydia and Caria (*Illiad*, 4.141-42), and Pliny the Elder going so far as to claim it was invented in the nearby Lydian town of Sardis (*Natural History*, 7.56.195). The other manufacturing method involved the use of the kermes-oak, either a plant or an insect. The lack of consistency in the results of dyeing meant that a range of colors such as violet, scarlet, and purple could be categorized as "purple," leading the first-century CE writer Pliny the Elder to observe:

> I note that the principal [luxury] colors are the three following: (1) red, as of the kermes-insect, which, from the lowliness of the dark rose, shades, if you look up at it in a bright light, into Tyrian purple, double-dyed purple and Laconian purple. (2) amethyst, which from violet itself passes into purple. . . . (3) The third belongs properly to the purple of the murex, but includes many kindred shades. (*Natural History*, 21.22.45-46, LCL)

In all cases, it is clear that Pliny associates the color purple with luxury.

Purple had a number of uses in Roman antiquity, but was primarily used by the elite of society. It was sometimes applied to a woman's cheeks or lips as a cosmetic, but by far the most important use of purple was in the clothes of the upper ranks. The toga, which only Roman citizens were allowed to wear, was given a purple border as a mark of distinction. While for most citizens the toga was plain white, families of men in the equestrian order had a narrow purple stripe along the border and senators and their families had a broad purple stripe on the border. Children of any status had togas with purple stripes along the edge, although at age fifteen they began to wear the plain white toga, unless of a high ranking family. Generals who were triumphant wore a completely purple toga, as did some later emperors.

In a description of a military triumph, a victory parade, led by the emperor Claudius, we find the following:

> His wife Messalina followed his chariot in a carriage, as
> did also those who had won the triumphal regalia in the
> same war; the rest marched on foot in purple-bordered
> togas, except Marcus Crassus Frugi, who rode a capari-
> soned horse and wore a tunic embroidered with palms,
> because he was receiving the honor for the second time.
> (Suetonius, *Claudius*, 17, LCL)

In another setting of honor, the funerary march, we find again
the presence of purple-bordered togas as a mark of distinction
and rank. Polybius notes how family members of the deceased
took special "ancestor masks" made in the image of predeceased
family members, and placed them

> on men who seem to them to bear the closest resemblance
> to the original in stature and carriage. These representatives
> wear togas, with a purple border if the deceased was a
> consul or praetor, whole purple if he was a censor, and
> embroidered with gold if he had collected a triumph or
> achieved anything similar.[12]

Rich and distinguished women were shrouded in purple wind-
ing sheets when they were being prepared for burial. Purple-
dyed coverings were used for dining couches and as a mark of
distinction and luxury at banquets. Some people, however,
seemed to go too far, as shown by Plutarch's (derisive) comments
on the boorish practices of Lucullus:

> [His] daily dinners were ostentatiously extravagant—not
> only their purple coverlets, beakers adorned with precious
> stones, choruses, and dramatic recitations, but also their
> display of all sorts of meats and daintily prepared dishes—
> making him an object of envy to the vulgar.[13]

Despite reserving purple for the rich and powerful, there are
some indications that purple was used by all social groups, not
just the wealthy. The finest kind of purple was reserved for ex-

clusive imperial usage, use by others being punished as a form of high treason. Nevertheless, since purple dye was manufactured and readily accessible in different grades of quality and color variation, the use of purple trimmed robes or robes dyed completely purple was quite common, much to the chagrin of the upper ranks of society. This was a matter of some people attempting publicly to display themselves as beyond their actual rank in society, yet another spin-off of Romanization among the lower ranks in their attempt to emulate the elite, as we discussed in chapter 3.

An examination of inscriptional evidence for those working with purple dye and purple goods in antiquity reveals that most mention groups of workers rather than individuals. This is not surprising, since most laborers in antiquity formed themselves into groups based on their common trade. These groups are known by various names in the inscriptions and ancient literature—there are so many designators that no single term will suffice to encapsulate all of them. In discussing these groups, scholars tend to call them by the most common of their Roman designators, *collegia*, or use the term "voluntary associations." This latter term is perhaps the most common, although it is not unproblematic. Bruce J. Malina has pointed out that the pressure to belong to one of these groups hardly makes them voluntary in the modern sense of the word, the more so if they are ethnically based or domestic in nature. While this is true, an individual could choose, often at his or her own peril, to withdraw from a group—two extreme examples being a *Ioudaios* undergoing *epispasm* to remove the mark of circumcision or a runaway household slave, such as Onesimus who clearly was not a Jesus believer when he left Philemon, despite the "conversion" of the household (Phlm 15-16). For this reason, these groups are better referred to with the awkwardly sounding but descriptively apropos term "elective social formations," since a person elects to join or withdraw and the groups are, at their core, social formations of people that evidence all of the behavior of group dynamics.

The existence of an association of purple dyers at Philippi is thought by some scholars to be confirmed by a fragmentary Latin inscription reading *PURPURAI* (*CIL* 3.664; the first two letters having been restored). An earlier, now lost, inscription found in 1872 reads "The city honored from among the purple dyers, an outstanding citizen, Antiochus, the son of Lykus, a native of Thyatira, as a benefactor." The authenticity of this inscription has been called into question, and unfortunately there is no way to authenticate it now that it is lost.[14] The poor state of preservation and the slow excavations of the site of Philippi itself leave little hope of finding further evidence, although perhaps one day more will be found.

On purple dyers in Macedonia more generally, however, we have a Greek inscription from Thessalonica dated to the second century CE, which reads, "The association of purple dyers of Eighteenth Street. In memory of Menippus, son of Amius, who is also called Severus, from Thyatira" (*IG* X/2 291). It is noteworthy that in this inscription, and perhaps even the disputed inscription from Philippi itself, we find mention of Thyatira, the city from which Lydia heralds, alongside a connection with purple. This reflects the economic importance of Thyatira, and the area of Lydia more generally, as a source of export of purple dye and purple-dyed goods, as we noted above. Unfortunately, the Thessalonian inscription does not provide enough information to determine whether or not any women were connected with the Thessalonian purple trade.

Other inscriptions attest to the purple trade, such as a married couple on the island of Cos who are both designated as purple dealers.[15] Latin uses of the term for purple dealer, *purpuraius/a*, are more frequent than the Greek term, and in many cases the groups of purple dealers are comprised of men and women, with women being numerous and in some cases even holding majority membership in the group. Overall, however, there is much less evidence for the involvement of women in elective social formations based on occupation than there is for men.

When one looks at evidence from elective social formations that seem to have had as their focus ritual enactments for a particular deity or set of deities, women played a larger role. In some cases women participated alongside men—while in other cases the group was composed entirely of women—and were involved in such groups independent from a *paterfamilias*, husband, or *kyrios*.[16] Among the scant inscriptional finds from associations at Philippi, one stone records a dedication by an association of "distinguished maenads," which suggests an all-female group.[17]

Overall, when one looks at the proportion of females to males involved in elective social formations, the females were vastly outnumbered. Nevertheless, that they were involved at all, especially in mixed gender or nondomestic settings, attests both to the relative freedoms attained by women in the first century and to the Romanization of these women in their concern for status display and social interaction similar to that of males. Again, we find in the social world of Paul's day evidence for the type of person Lydia would have been—an independent woman working in the trade of a luxury good and supporting others, perhaps even being benefactor to an elective social formation, through her income.

CHAPTER 5

Lydia in Ritual Space

I t is important to remember that at the time of Lydia and Paul, what we call religion was actually part of the kinship or political systems. There was domestic religion and political religion—but no religion, pure and simple, differentiated from the kin group or the *polis*. When we ask about where to locate Lydia on the map of religious affiliations in antiquity, we are in fact asking about the deities shown reverence (that is, worshiped) within her household or city. Household worship recognized the traditional deities of one's ancestors, the ancestors themselves, local household deities (*Lares*), as well as specialized deities who may have been of particular help to the worshiper. Given this array of deities, the question of Lydia's domestic and/or political religion is a difficult problem. Luke is at his vaguest when writing his brief note about her, and a few anomalies in the passage have caused no shortage of controversy. Most of the controversy hinges on how one understands two key phrases in Acts 16: the reference to Lydia being a "worshiper of God" (*sebomenē ton theon*, 16:14) and the reference to the meeting at a "place of prayer" (*proseuchē*, 16:13, 16). In order to do justice to the varying scholarly opinions around these phrases, we will present the most commonly proposed scenarios concerning Lydia's religious commitments, and the evidence used to support particular understandings of the passage. Although we will begin by looking at the location of Lydia's meeting with Paul and then turn to Luke's description of Lydia's religious affiliation, these two aspects of the passage are difficult to keep completely separate and thus there will be some overlap in our discussion.

Lydia as a Worshiper of God

Luke writes that Lydia was a "worshiper of God" (*sebomenē ton theon*, Acts 16:14). Many commentators understand this phrase to indicate that Lydia was a non-*Ioudaios* participant in synagogue worship, or at least sympathetic to the monotheism of the *Ioudaioi*. In and of itself, the verb *sebomai*, along with its substantive forms, does not indicate Jewish cult but is simply a reference to ritual piety—one finds the word used elsewhere in Acts for the worship of the goddess Artemis at Ephesus (19:27). What gives pause with reference to Lydia is the appellation *ton theon* ("[of] the God"), which implies henotheism, the worship of one deity at the expense of all others.[1] A phrase such as "worshiper of God" was not often used to refer to *Ioudaioi*; it was perhaps applied to non-*Ioudaioi* by the *Ioudaioi* as a label for those who had some level of attraction, affiliation, or adherence to Israelite religion. At the same time, such people had not converted to Judaism, thus becoming proselytes (*prosēlytos*). Indeed, the paucity of evidence for formal conversion to Judaism in the first century CE, and the vague turns of phrases such as this one in scattered sources, continues to generate considerable debate over the nature of Jewish sympathizers—non-*Ioudaioi* who not only had some interaction with the Jewish community but expressed some sort of attachment to the practices and/or the beliefs of that community. These sympathizers, sometimes also referred to as "God-fearers," are attested in a few epigraphic and literary sources in antiquity, although the primary evidence for their existence comes from the book of Acts where we find references to "worshipers of God" (Acts 16:14; 18:7; cf. 18:13), the "devout" of the synagogue (Acts 17:4, 17), and "fearers of God" (Acts 10:2, 22; 13:16, 26; cf. 10:35).

In the past, these "God-fearers," as they have come to be called, were treated as a well-defined group of Gentiles who affiliated with a synagogue, accepted henotheism, and took on many, but not all, customs and practices by keeping to food regulations and Sabbath rest, but by foregoing ritual circumcision (in the case of males). That is, they clearly expressed a desire to worship the "one true God" but had not fully converted. The absolutizing of the category of "God-fearer" as being the same in every place and at every time in the first few centuries of the Common Era led other scholars to reject outright their existence, at least in the first century, charging Luke with fabricating the category as a literary device to help his hero, Paul, bridge the world of the *Ioudaioi* and the world of the Gentiles.[2]

At present, scholars working in this area are reaching a compromise that recognizes the existence of first-century Gentiles who expressed varying degrees of attachment to the synagogue and its customary way of life. There is no evidence of formal recognition of Gentiles before the second century CE, at least before the implementation of the *fiscus judaicus* in 96 CE, a tax levied on all *Ioudaioi* by the Roman authorities, which necessitated *Ioudaioi* and Romans alike to know who was and who was not a *Ioudaios*. Much of this has not, unfortunately, filtered down into the commentary literature, and one continues to find references to Lydia, whom Luke designates as a "worshiper of God," as a "God-fearer," with subsequent descriptions that detail her piety toward the Jewish God and her reluctance to fully commit to becoming a *Ioudaios*. Accordingly, it is only through Jesus, as presented by Paul, that Lydia comes to see how she can fully accept the Jewish God without the "trappings" of Judaism.

Such views do a disservice to Lydia and to Judaism. The variability in what being a "God-fearer" means allows for the possibility of multiple interpretations of Lydia's status. She could have been like Julia Severa, a Gentile woman living in the city of Acmonia in the mid-first century CE, who was honored by a Jewish community for her benefaction in constructing a meeting place (*oikos*) for the *Ioudaioi*. The inscription reads, in part, "The synagogue honors these individuals with a gold shield on account of their excellent leadership and their kindly feelings toward and zeal for the congregation" (*CIJ* 2.766). Julia Severa is also known from local coins, which recognize her holding the position of high priestess of the local imperial cult. We are led to conclude that she enjoyed a close relationship with the local Jewish community, and was recognized for her support, while still holding office in a cult that ran counter to the very core of Jewish beliefs.[3]

We find another example in an early-first-century inscription from Berenice that honors a Roman official, Marcus Tittius, for his support of the Jewish community as well as for his kindness to the Greek citizens of the city.[4] In this case, his benefaction toward the *Ioudaioi* did not, we assume, necessitate his withdrawal from politics, despite the nature of polytheist cultic activity that would have been associated with civic duty (something we can safely assume for the "God-fearer" Cornelius in Acts 10–11, for whom the position of Roman centurion would have necessitated recognition of the Roman gods, but for whom benefaction toward the local *Ioudaioi* garnered him honorific recognition by Luke).[5] We can see, then, that being a fearer or worshiper of God allowed for a great diversity of practice and belief among Gentiles who were linked to local Jewish communities to different degrees and for different reasons, not simply philosophic or religious ones.

Strikingly, while Paul and his companions speak to the women, only one of them is designated as a "worshiper of God." Elsewhere Luke takes care to describe those listening to Paul, usually designating them as *Ioudaioi* and/or Gentiles, occasionally adding the reference to fearers or worshipers of God. In those cases, however, Luke spells out for his readers the affiliations of the whole audience, and whenever Paul attends a synagogue the Jewish connection is made explicit in every instance without exception (see Acts 13:5, 14-16; 14:1; 17:1, 10, 17; 18:4; 19:8-10). This is not the case in our passage, where only Lydia is designated a "God-worshiper." We are not given any indication of the religious commitments of any of her female companions, whether each is a *Ioudaios*, Gentile, sympathizer, or fearer, again marking a break with Luke's pattern throughout the rest of the narrative. Before we draw any final conclusions, however, we need to return to the passage in Acts, since scholarly understanding of Lydia as a "God-worshiper" or "God-fearer" is linked to the interpretation of Luke's use of the word *proseuchē* as "place of prayer for *Ioudaioi*," an understanding that is equally problematic and controversial as "God-worshiper," as we shall see.

Places of Prayer

Luke begins the narrative specifically about Lydia with a verbatim first-person quotation from one of his sources: "On the sabbath day we went outside the gate by the river, where we supposed there was a place of prayer [*proseuchē*]; and we sat down and spoke to the women who had gathered there" (Acts 16:13). On another day they again head out to the same place, which is again designated as a *proseuchē* (Acts 16:16). Two things are immediately clear.[6] First, this is not an accidental or ad hoc gathering since the verb used here implies a sense of a community gathering for a specific purpose. Second, the references to sitting and speaking indicate that the location is a ritual space in which teaching and interpretation are among the cultic actions taking place.[7]

Many commentators have suggested that the meeting that Paul and his companions discovered was a gathering of adherents to Judaism, as we noted above on the use of "worshiper of God." The second piece of evidence in this argument is Luke's use of *proseuchē*. In the Greek-speaking Diaspora *proseuchē* was the main official designation for a building dedicated to Jewish practices, according to Jewish and non-Jewish sources. Some commentators thus conclude that Luke is using *proseuchē* to refer to a physical building, and not simply a particular location. Other commentators recognize that *proseuchē* can also indicate outdoor meetings, the most likely sense in this case, albeit still a Jewish worship service.[8]

Another proposal has most recently been put forward by Bruce J. Malina and John J. Pilch, who argue that Lydia and her household were not [fully-]observant Israelites. They point out that the phrase "fearers of God" appears frequently in the Septuagint to describe members of the house of Israel who acknowledge the one God. The phrase, however, includes "those assimilated Israelites who neglected circumcision and/or did not observe Torah in its entirety."[9] Malina and Pilch understand the *proseuchē* as a place where the Israelites gathered as a group to pray, the riverside location providing a ready supply of water for ablutions, which were of particular interest to women (here they reference Josephus, *Jewish Antiquities*, 14.20.23 and Lev 15:19-23). Although it is not fully clear why they think Lydia is a somewhat nonobservant Israelite (perhaps simply because Luke does not refer to her as a *"Ioudaios"*), this is an innovative if controversial suggestion that invites more investigation.

A third proposal, the one to which I find myself drawn, suggests that Lydia is neither Jewish nor a Gentile attracted to Judaism. Luke's vague language reflects his attempt to bring Lydia's story into conformity with his pattern of having Paul and his companions go first to the synagogue and then to the Gentiles. In every other city this is Paul's pattern. It is striking that the only time Luke breaks this pattern is where he switches to the first-person narration, which suggests that he has an eyewitness source for the Philippian visit. While Luke does not deny that the women at the riverside gathering were Jewish, he does not clearly say it either. A Jewish reader might have recognized in words like *proseuchē* and "God-worshiper" affiliation with

Judaism to some degree. Yet these words equally could have been understood by non-*Ioudaioi* as referring to a place in which any of the gods were worshiped, and that Lydia was devout in carrying out religious rituals.

That it was not a synagogue meeting in this instance is clear, as only women were in attendance, not the ten adult males who were required by tradition for the establishment of a synagogue (the *minyan*, or "quorum").[10] And while it is the case that the word *proseuchē* is used for a Jewish place of prayer it is also used of non-Jewish places of ritual activity where no Jewish influence is possible. Luke does not mention that there actually was a gathering of *Ioudaioi* or even a gathering of "worshipers of God" by the river even when Paul and the others arrived there—as we noted above, only Lydia is so designated. Furthermore, even if *proseuchē* is taken to indicate a gathering of *Ioudaioi*, Luke only notes that Paul and his companions "supposed" that this was a *proseuchē*—he does not confirm that this was the case by giving other indications of the Jewish nature of the meeting. The characters' "supposition" fits well, however, with Luke's presentation of Paul going first to the *Ioudaioi* and then to the Gentiles, a recruitment strategy that Paul himself does not mention in his letters (for example, see Acts 13:5, 14; 14:1; 17:1, 10; 18:1-4, 19). The very placing of the initial contact "on the sabbath day" is probably added by Luke, as the notion that Jesus and his followers observed the Sabbath is certainly a Lukan one (see Luke 4:31; 6:6; 13:10; 23:56; Acts 17:2; 18:4).

In presenting the case for Lydia's involvement not only in a Jewish meeting, but one that takes place in a physical building, a synagogue, Ivoni Richter Reimer argues the following:

> Dirty work done in dye works and tanneries also had to be conducted outside the city because of the stink it produced. According to Pliny, the production of purple cloth by the use of vegetable dyes is also a filthy (*sordidum*) job. On this basis, we can discern a deeper meaning in Acts 16:13: synagogue buildings were located in the vicinity of

the people who belonged to them. Moreover, a good deal
of water was needed for working with purple.[11]

This quote, however, betrays an inconsistency grounded in
Reimer's desire to have the *proseuchē* bear too much weight in
her argument. All of her data are correct; it is the combination of
the data that leads to her conclusion that is problematic. It is true
that some production facilities, such as dyeing, were located
outside town gates (and downwind), and it is true that water
was needed for dyeing. Thus, the place where the women were
gathered would have fit with the location of dyeing production.
It is also true that synagogue buildings were located in proximity
to the inhabitants who used them. Here, however, Reimer has
made two unjustified leaps in logic. First, Reimer assumes that
Lydia was involved in the production of dyed cloth. This is not
at all clear, and it may well have been the case that Lydia's mer-
chandise was already dyed or that she dealt in the dye itself, thus
obviating the need for water. Reimer's second leap is that there
is an actual building involved. This is not likely for a small group
such as she proposes for Lydia, since a dedicated synagogue
building would not have been feasible, if at all desirable because,
at best, they were "worshipers of god" and not Jewish. If it were
a building, it more likely would have been inside the city, close
to where the people lived, not outside the gate. If, as is more
probable in a place such as Philippi that had a small (if any!)
Jewish population, the local gathering of *Ioudaioi* (literally, the
"*synagogē*," which is at its linguistic core a reference to the people
not a building) took place in a home such as Lydia's we would
not likely find it outside the city walls. So, while I can agree with
Reimer's locating the gathering place outside the city walls as
perhaps linked to the production of dyed material, I cannot agree
that it is also a synagogue, or even the most natural place for a
Jewish meeting. This simply does not fit with what we know
about Jewish gatherings elsewhere in the first century.

In light of Luke's redactional tendencies and his choice of
language it seems to me that he has embellished a tradition of

Paul's first contacts at Philippi. Luke has at his disposal a tradition of a devout woman who became Paul's first recruit in Philippi. Within the context of Luke's writing, there are hints that Lydia was an adherent of things Jewish, but Luke's choice of not one but two unclear references—"worshiper of God" and "place of prayer"—leave it unclear as to the full nature of Lydia's religious commitments. She may well worship a deity or deities alongside or even other than the God of Israel. Even if she did worship the God of Israel, it is not clear that her companions shared her status as "worshiper of God." All that can be stated with any certainty is that Paul and company encountered a group of women gathered for the worship of a deity.

My own interpretation, albeit not one that is widely shared, is that Luke has deliberately used vague terms here because his first-person sources indicate that at Philippi Paul's first contact was with non-*Ioudaioi*, but Luke does not want to completely disrupt his pattern of having Paul go first to the *Ioudaioi* and then to the Gentiles. While it is true that the attraction of eastern cults throughout the Roman Empire would certainly have brought some inquisitors to Judaism, there were other cults that would have proven particularly attractive to the women at Philippi. It will serve us well to consider briefly what other religious affiliations were available to Lydia at Philippi.

Women and Cults at Philippi

Roman domestic and political religions were focused primarily on concerns about the will of the gods and what the gods could do for one's economic and social standing. Cicero, writing in the mid–first century BCE, encapsulates the core of Roman religious attitudes when he asks:

> Did anyone ever render thanks to the gods because he was
> a good man? No, because he was rich, honored, secure. The
> reason why men give to Jupiter the titles of Best and Great-

est is not that they think that he makes us just, temperate or wise, but safe, secure, wealthy and opulent. (*On the Nature of the Gods*, 3.36.87, LCL)

The Romans did not look to the gods to provide moral guidance—that was the purview of the philosophers. If one wanted to know whether or not the gods favored a particular course of action, however, one would approach the priests and diviners of the gods (Cicero, *On Divination*, 2.4.10-11). Cicero's code of laws for religious behavior set out, in idealized fashion, the general tenor of religious expectations, at least among elite Romans:

They shall approach the gods in purity, bringing piety and leaving riches behind. Whoever shall do otherwise, heaven itself will deal out punishment to him. No one shall have gods to himself, either new gods or alien gods, unless recognized by the state. Privately they shall worship those gods whose worship they have duly received from their ancestors. . . . In cities they shall have shrines; they shall have groves in the country and homes for the *Lares*. . . . They shall preserve the rites of their families and their ancestors. (*Laws*, 2.8.19-20, LCL)

Cicero's views reflect attitudes about the traditional Roman religions that supported and were supported by the state. There was, however, another aspect to religion that was being imported from the eastern empire.

In the Hellenistic age and even more so in the Roman period, the propensity grew for worship experiences that entailed alternate states of consciousness (often called "mystic" cults). This propensity was probably due to the contact of western peoples with these eastern practices through war, trade, and travel. That women were predominantly attracted to the worship of foreign deities is exemplified by Plutarch's slur concerning their enticement by the priests of the Great Mother and of Sarapis (*Moralia*, 407c). Deities originally located in the east flourished in Philippi, and a number of open shrines have been found in the rock of the acropolis. These are dedicated to various Eastern gods including Sylvanus, Artemis, Bendis, Cybele, and Dionysus. Ruins of a sanctuary of the Egyptian gods dedicated to the worship of Isis, Sarapis, and Harpocrates have also been unearthed. At Philippi, the sanctuary of Diana, the Roman goddess of woodland and wild nature and the protector of women (associated with the Greek goddess Artemis), is linked to rock reliefs of Diana, each about one square foot, cut into the hillside of the acropolis. On the nearly two hundred reliefs on the hill, forty priestesses are depicted.[12] Such evidence suggests not only the popularity of the cult among women during the time of Paul and his successors, but also the prominent place held by women within the hierarchy of the administration of this worship form (the same holds true of the worship of Isis at Philippi).

The cult of Dionysus, the god of wine, fertility, and liberated emotions (also called Bacchus), was widespread in Hellenistic and Roman times. Devotees of Dionysus were mostly women in the early Hellenistic period, although toward the first century BCE males were included in the rites, particularly those who were members of theatrical troops. Five inscriptions related to the cult of Dionysus found in Philippi list a number of women who had donated votive offerings of significant amounts. These inscriptions indicate that "these women had a remarkable degree of economic independence, which can be explained by the fact that they enjoyed complete control over their money."[13]

During the time of Lydia, there existed in Philippi a number of imperial cult sites, particularly those dedicated to Augustus and Livia, and probably also Claudius.[14] Such sites likely involved women as officiants. In her study of inscriptional evidence for women's religion in Italy, Amy Richlin notes that of eighty-four women given the title *sacerdose* (or priestess) about 29% were involved in the imperial cult.[15] As with the other cults she examines, such as Magna Mater, Ceres, Venus, and Isis, women associated with the imperial cult tended to be freeborn women and more than half were from the elite. As we have already noted, however, the elite women led the way for the majority of nonelite women, who would have found themselves in a better position to take on cultic leadership roles on the strength of the example of the rich and famous.

After the Battle of Philippi (42 BCE) in which Antony and Octavian defeated Brutus and Cassius, Antony settled his veterans and supporters in Philippi and placed the city under the protection of Isis. Many of the veterans' families would have remembered that in 34 BCE Antony presented the spoils of his triumph over the Armenians to Cleopatra instead of presenting them to Capitoline Jupiter. At the time of the presentation Cleopatra sat on a throne in the garb of Isis, an identity she continued to develop.[16] During the first century of the Common Era the cult of Isis was one of the most important of the eastern cults in Philippi. It too had a history of women leaders, both in the public temples and in private elective social formations.

The attraction of eastern cults among the women of Philippi and the widespread participation of women as leaders in these cults sets the context in which to understand the attraction of Jesus for Lydia and her household. One need not posit Judaism as the intermediary, although it too would have been among the eastern cults that proved attractive in the Roman west. In and of itself, however, Jesus worship would have been understood among the eastern cults that were disseminating ideas of a dominant deity and heretofore unknown rituals and beliefs. The promise of an afterlife, and a good one at that, was not the sole possession of the Jesus cult, as other cults held out similar offers. Nevertheless, it was the Jesus cult that caught the attention of Lydia, whereas Diana proved attractive among other women at Philippi, and Isis or Dionysus among still other women. Whether or not a first stage adherence to Judaism (as a "worshiper of God") was involved in Lydia's case, it is clear that she would not have been alone among the women of the *kolōnia* in finding eastern cults attractive and becoming involved in hosting and leading a group of cult devotees in her home.

Not only does Lydia's leadership fit into the patterns of women's participation in cult life in Philippi, it fits into Paul's network of colleagues and coworkers. In the letters of Paul we find a number of places where women are referred to, often in passing, as working with Paul. The passing nature of the comments should not cause us to think that these women were unimportant or that Paul did not value their leadership. Rather, the brevity of the references suggests that Paul felt no need to defend the right of women in leadership in the Jesus communities nor did he expect any opposition to their presence.

Since women played a key public and social role at Philippi, it is thus not surprising to find evidence that women had prominent roles among the Jesus group at that same city in Paul's letter to the Philippians. That Paul used a public letter to appeal for reconciliation between Euodia and Syntyche (Phil 4:2-3) suggests that their conflict was more than a matter of a private difference of opinion. Since their differences had ramifications for the entire group, it is more likely that it concerned a question of belief, worship, or conduct. Paul did not suppress the rights of each of these two women to express themselves; he only asked that their differences be resolved.

Elsewhere we hear of Chloe, the leader of a house group at Corinth (1 Cor 1:11), and Phoebe, Paul's patron and a deacon of the Jesus group at Cenchrea (Rom 16:1-2). Prisca, along with her husband Aquila (although Prisca is named first by Paul, giving her higher honor) are called coworkers (Rom 16:3) and were hosts for a Jesus group somewhere in Asia Minor, perhaps in Ephesus (1 Cor 16:19; cf. 2 Tim 4:19). This wife and husband team seem to have traveled to different places where they were involved in the Jesus groups (Acts 18:2, 18), even teaching and correcting Apollos, who himself became a leader among the Corinthians (Acts 18:26; 1 Cor 1:12, 3:6, 16:12). Paul describes Junia as being "prominent among the apostles" (Rom 16:7), which many commentators understand to mean that she herself bore the title "apostle." Paul notes that Mary worked hard among the Roman Jesus believers (Rom 16:6), as did Tryphaena and Tryphosa, who are singled out as "workers in the Lord" (Rom 16:12). Julia, Olympas, and the unnamed sister of Nereus are selected from among the believers alongside a few honorable men, and thus can be assumed to have been of equal status (Rom 16:15).[17]

These women represent only a few examples of what must surely have been a greater number of women among Paul's wide network of colleagues and coworkers. Even these few, however, demonstrate that Paul considered women equal to men in undertaking the propagation of the Jesus cult in urban centers in the Roman world. It is among such women that we find Lydia the purple dealer, the first person to host a Jesus group on Greek soil and the center of a network through which the Jesus cult spread in Philippi, so that the group to whom Paul writes is credited with "sharing in the gospel from the first day until now" (Phil 1:5, cf. 4:15).

CONCLUSION

Once Paul and his companions leave Philippi Lydia and her house-based community disappear from the narrative, as is the case with so many of Luke's characters. Even when Paul later passes through Philippi (Acts 20:6) there is no mention of Lydia. Likewise, in Paul's letter to the Philippians Lydia gets no mention. Nevertheless, evidence from a number of early Jesus-group writings and archaeological remains from Philippi give the impression that women continued to play an important role in the life of the Jesus group at Philippi. We have already noted the mention of Euodia and Syntyche by Paul (Phil 4:2-3). Another letter written to the Philippian Jesus community came from the hand of Polycarp of Smryna, written approximately 98–117 CE. There are hints in this letter that Polycarp was aware of the freedom and respect that the Philippian women enjoyed, something with which he himself was not entirely happy, since he insists that women act with proper "decorum." Such attitudes were in keeping with the social attitude that (re)developed in Roman society toward the end of the first century, largely in reaction to the "new" women that arose out of the Augustan reforms.

Another small piece of evidence for the continuing public role of women at Philippi comes from a fragmentary portion of the apocryphal *Acts of Paul*, written in the latter part of the second century CE, in which Fortuna, a woman of Philippi, is brought to faith in Jesus by Paul and is killed by her father as a result.[1] Miraculously, Paul brings her back to life, causing a crowd of nonbelievers, representative of the entire city of Philippi, to come to believe. Part of this document's agenda was the promotion of asceticism and the freedom it brings to Jesus-group women. Set in the mid-first century but written in the late-second century, it shows in a cursory fashion that women continued to be well-known in the traditions about the Philippian Jesus community. Women continued to play a prominent role in church leadership through the Byzantine period, at least until the sixth century. Graves associated with the basilicas in Philippi refer to women as deacons (using the masculine form of the word, *diakonos*, even after the feminine form of the word, *diakonissa*, came into use in the third or fourth century), canonesses (*kaononikē*), and servants (*doulos* or *servus*, used for both men and women), although no woman is attested as having reached the highest position of presbyter.[2]

The poor state of preservation in the archaeological record at Philippi makes it difficult to know to what degree Lydia was venerated there. The city itself continued in its prosperity into the post–Constantine era, when it became a place of pilgrimage and had a distinctly Christian center. Four large church sites have been identified. In the area of the Market Hall the remains of an octagon church have been discovered, so named due to its internal octagonal colonnade. The church itself dates to the early-fifth century, but was built on an earlier basilica site. An inscription in a mosaic floor within these remains identifies the earlier building as the "basilica of Paul," which was paid for by a local bishop named Porphyrios, who held the seat from 312–42 CE. The initial building on the site, dating to the second century BCE, was a barrel-vaulted tomb of Euephenes, son of Exekestos, later developed into a site of a hero cult during the Roman period. Christians replaced the memorial to this hero with one to their own hero—Paul—although it is not clear whether in doing so they intended to erase the hero's memory or respect it by absorbing his cult site into their own. By the sixth century CE the octagon church had undergone significant alterations and was part of a much larger ecclesiastical complex. Also around the mid-sixth century a large basilica was constructed adjacent to the Palaestra (called Basilica B), although the sanctuary dome collapsed before the building was completed. Basilica A stands on the north side of the Via Egnatia and dates from around 500 CE. A small crypt from Roman times located by its southwest corner is the reputed site of Paul's imprisonment (cf. Acts 16:24). A short distance to the east is Basilica C, dating from the fourth to sixth century. These buildings reflect a rich Christian tradition at Philippi, but too little is known about them to determine what part, if any, the veneration of Lydia played in these locations.

Lydia was recognized very early on in the church as a saint and her feast day is celebrated on August 3. Today, adjacent to the ruins at Philippi, the Greek Orthodox Baptistery of St. Lydia overlooks a modern baptismal area at the Krenides River. The baptistery is richly decorated with iconographic depictions of Lydia and Paul and the site remains a pilgrimage destination as the place where Lydia was baptized. It is a possible location, but it offers more for modern piety than it does for a historical reconstruction for the life of Lydia in mid-first-century Philippi.

In our study of Lydia we have moved from the general to the particular. We began by examining the civic contexts with which Lydia was affiliated, both of which were highly Romanized, although Philippi much more so than Thyatira. We then turned our attention to women in the domestic sphere and the types of opportunities available to them, or not, during the mid-first century. Luke's information about Lydia allowed us to place her with women who had found freedom from their guardians, their *kyrios*, and were able to take care of their own affairs and run their own households. A consequence of this was Lydia's ability to offer hospitality to Paul and his companions and to become host, and perhaps patron, to the Jesus group at Philippi. In the marketplace women were generally linked to the honor of their family, either through their husbands or their *paterfamilias*. Augustan marriage reforms, however, had opened up new opportunities for women to participate in public life. As a consequence, women could enter into the workforce, primarily as artisans or commercial operators, most often in industry linked to the domestic sphere, above all the clothing industry. It is in this area that we find Lydia, a merchant trader of purple dye or dyed goods. Finally, we noted Lydia's involvement in ritual space, wrestling with the thorny issues of what is behind Luke's labels "worshiper of God" and "place of prayer." At the very least, Lydia bears the marks of a pious woman, taking leadership of a group formed for ritual, as did so many women of Philippi before and after her.

In summary, we used the scant evidence from the book of Acts alongside social-scientific models and historical patterns to sketch out what Lydia's life would have looked like in different social spheres. In so doing, we found indications that allowed us to plot the social networks available to Lydia insofar as they were available to some women during the mid-first century CE. This allowed us to see how Lydia, despite her upbringing in the eastern part of the Roman Empire, fell into the patterns of Romanization that were taking place from the Augustan age. This is no surprise given that she was living in an urban center, especially one as heavily Romanized as was Philippi.

In the end, I imagine Lydia as a Romanized immigrant living in Philippi, well-off, but not elite, involved in ritual piety and expressing all the typical patterns of householder hospitality one would expect in antiquity. To arrive at this construction I have used social-scientific modeling, as well as classical historical exegesis of the passage, and no small part of my own historic imagination. Many are sure to fault me on the latter, critiquing my particular construction of Lydia. And they may be correct. Yet in reading other presentations of Lydia in the secondary literature, my portrait is no less a construction than that of others, and perhaps somewhat better than the idealized hagiography of later iconographic depictions of Lydia in art. In many aspects, it is different from usual depictions of Lydia, as I have attempted to highlight in the preceding chapters, but it is neither better nor worse for that. It simply attempts to use the most recent methods and data available to construct as good a portrait as may be done. It is offered here as part of the wider dialogue not only on the identity of Lydia but on the social makeup of the network of friends and colleagues affiliated with Paul and his vision to bring the gospel of God to the northeastern Mediterranean region of the Greco-Roman world.

NOTES

Notes to Introduction (pages 1–13)

1. Comparison among the first three gospels is called "redaction criticism" and is a method that has been used for many decades in establishing the theologies and writing styles of the gospel writers. Although we do not have the sources for John's gospel or for Acts, it is clear that the writers of both documents used sources, and so redaction criticism is also the term used for the attempt to uncover the nature of these sources. The sifting of layers in Acts is described by Gerd Lüdemann, *Early Christianity According to the Traditions in Acts: A Commentary* (Minneapolis, MN: Fortress, 1989), 19–23 and throughout. A thoroughgoing and vigorous redactional analysis of Acts 16:11-15, 40 is undertaken by Jean-Pierre Sterck-Degueldre, *Eine Frau namens Lydia*, WUNT II/176 (Tübingen: Mohr Siebeck, 2004), 42–195. For a discussion of the issues involved in the interpretation of the "we passages" in Acts, see Ben Witherington III, *The Acts of the Apostles: A Socio-Rhetorical Commentary* (Grand Rapids, MI: Eerdmans, 1998), 480–86. Peter Pilhofer argues that the writer of Acts is the "man from Macedonia" of Paul's nighttime vision (Acts 16:9) and was a resident of Philippi, thus the details of Paul at Philippi are historically reliable (*Philippi*, Band I. *Die erste christliche Gemeinde Europas*, WUNT 87 [Tübingen: Mohr Siebeck, 1995], 156–59), a position with which Sterck-Degueldre does not agree, arguing that Luke has here used a travel source (*Eine Frau namens Lydia*, 40), although he does maintain the veracity of the account and the historical reliability of the details concerning Lydia.

2. The Greek term that is used in Acts 16:14—*porphyropōlis*—quite literally indicates "dealer in purple" and thus can indicate a dealer in cloth dyed purple but also can have wider connotations, such as indicating a person who deals more generally in goods dyed purple, or even trading in the purple dye itself.

3. See Bruce J. Malina, *Timothy: Paul's Closest Associate*, Paul's Social Network: Brothers and Sisters in Faith (Collegeville, MN: Liturgical Press, 2008), 53–62.

4. On Lydia's servile status, see G. H. R. Horsley, *New Documents Illustrating Early Christianity 2: A Review of the Greek Inscriptions and Papyri Published in 1977*, NewDocs 2 (Macquarie, Australia: The Ancient History Documentary Research Centre, Macquarie University, 1982), 27. Pilhofer concludes that "Lydia" is her ethnic name (i.e., "the Lydian") and suggests that she may be referred to by another name, perhaps even Euodia or Syntyche of Phil 4:2 (*Philippi* I, 236–37). Counter evidence is presented by Colin J. Hemer, "The Cities of Revelation," in *New Documents Illustrating Early Christianity 3*, ed. G. H. R. Horsley, NewDocs 3 (Macquarie, Australia: The Ancient History Documentary Research Centre, Macquarie University, 1983), 54; cf. Lüdemann (*Early Christianity*, 183) who also doubts that she came from Lydia. On citizenship, see Amy Richlin, "Carrying Water in a Sieve: Class and the Body in Roman Women's Religion," in *Women and Goddess Traditions: In Antiquity and Today*, ed. Karen L. King (Minneapolis, MN: Fortress, 1997), 358.

5. Robert A. Wortham, "The Problem of Anti-Judaism in 1 Thess 2:14-16 and Related Pauline Texts," *BTB* 25 (1995): 37.

6. Bruce J. Malina, "Understanding New Testament Persons," in *The Social Sciences and New Testament Interpretation*, ed. Richard L. Rohrbaugh (Peabody, MA: Hendrickson, 1996), 45.

7. Louise J. Lawrence, *Reading with Anthropology: Exhibiting Aspects of New Testament Religion* (Milton Keynes: Paternoster, 2005), 11.

8. Information on the following chart is a summary of various sources, although primarily H. C. Triandis, *Individualism and Collectivism* (Boulder, CO: Westview Press, 1995) and Geert Hofstede, "Foreword," in *Individualism and Collectivism: Theory, Method, and Applications*, eds. U. Kim, H. C. Triandis, C. Kagitcibasi, S.-C. Choi, and G. Yoon (Thousand Oaks, CA: Sage, 1994), ix–xiv. Very good summary descriptions of collectivism are provided in companion volumes in the Paul's Social Network series by Malina, *Timothy*, 1–20, and John J. Pilch, *Stephen: Paul and the Hellenist Israelites* (Collegeville, MN: Liturgical Press, 2008), 17–35.

9. Support for the research and writing of this book has been provided in part through a Government of Ontario Premier's Research Excellence Award (PREA) and a Social Sciences and Humanities Research Council of Canada (SSHRC) Standard Research Grant. I am grateful to my research assistant, Barbara Adle, for her work on some initial research for this project.

Notes to Chapter 1 (pages 15–27)

1. Richard L. Rohrbaugh, "The Preindustrial City," in *The Social Sciences and New Testament Interpretation*, ed. Richard L. Rohrbaugh (Peabody, MA: Hendrickson, 1996), 108–9, which includes the quotation from Pausanias on p. 109.

2. See further T. R. S. Broughton, "Roman Asia," in *An Economic Survey of Ancient Rome*, ed. Tenny Frank, vol. 4 (Baltimore, MD: Johns Hopkins University Press, 1938), 818–22; Colin J. Hemer, *The Letters to the Seven Churches of Asia in Their Local Setting*, JSNTSup 11 (Sheffield: Sheffield Academic Press, 1986), 109; W. M. Ramsay, *The Letters to the Seven Churches*, ed. Mark W. Wilson, updated ed. (Peabody, MA: Hendrickson, 1994), 238.

3. Although Paul Collart's *Philippes, ville de Macédonia, depuis ses origines jusqu'à la fin de la l'époque romaine*, Thèse, Université de Genève 85 (Paris: Boccard, 1937) remains a standard reference work for the city of Philippi, it has been thoroughly updated by the two-volume German work of Peter Pilhofer, who has summarized most of the earlier studies and collected information from diverse and scattered archaeological reports, supplemented by his own work done on site: *Philippi*, Band I, *Die erste christliche Gemeinde Europas*, WUNT 87 (Tübingen: Mohr Siebeck, 1995); and *Philippi*, Band II, *Katalog der Inschriften von Philippi*, WUNT 119 (Tübingen: Mohr Siebeck, 2000). Also important for the history of Philippi are Fanoula Papazoglou, "Macedonia Under the Romans," in *Macedonia: 4000 Years of Greek History and Civilization*, ed. M. B. Sakellariou (Athens: Ekdotike Athenon S.A., 1983), 192–207; and Ioannis Touratsoglou, *Macedonia: History, Monuments, Museum* (Athens: Ekdotike Athenon, 1995). The following summary is largely indebted to these sources.

4. For the detailed argument see Richard S. Ascough, "Civic Pride at Philippi: The Text-Critical Problem of Acts 16.12," *NTS* 44 (1996): 94–103.

5. Chaido Koukouli-Chrysantaki, "Colonia Iulia Augusta Philippensis," in *Philippi at the Time of Paul and After His Death*, eds. Charalambos Bakirtzis and Helmut Koester (Harrisburg, PA: Trinity Press International, 1998), 21.

6. Pilhofer, *Philippi* I, 91, 86; Koukouli-Chrysantaki, "Colonia," 23.

7. Joseph H. Hellerman, *Reconstructing Honor in Roman Philippi: Carmen Christi as* Cursus Pudorum, SNTSMS 132 (Cambridge: Cambridge University Press, 2005), 66.

8. Ibid.

9. Peter Oakes, *Philippians: From People to Letter*, SNTSMS 110 (Cambridge: Cambridge University Press, 2001), 34. Much of the following outline of the social makeup of the colony of Philippi in the mid-first century, and the makeup of the early Jesus group there, relies on the excellent social-scientific work of Oakes, *Philippians*, 1–54. His model is grounded in tracing the development of the colony from its founding in 42 BCE to the middle of the first century CE.

10. Ibid., 18, 50, 53–54. I have adjusted Oakes's summary to better reflect the nominal figures he presents on p. 17, fig. 10, and other information he presents throughout his book (reflected in my chart below).

11. Ibid., 45. Pilhofer's estimate is lower, at 5,000–10,000 (*Philippi* I, 76). As Oakes points out, either way he and Pilhofer are "talking about the same class of town size" (*Philippians*, 45).

12. See Oakes, *Philippians*, 27–28, 33; Hellerman, *Reconstructing Honor*, 71. The disappearance of the local elite is in contrast to colonization in other cities, where some of these elite were incorporated into the body of Roman citizens.

13. Oakes, *Philippians*, 54.

14. Hellerman, *Reconstructing Honor*, 71.

Notes to Chapter 2 (pages 28–57)

1. I have used here the Greek word *Ioudaioi* in place of the usual English translation "Jews." Of late there has been considerable scholarly debate over how best to render the singular *Ioudaios* and the plural *Ioudaioi* into English, with some scholars challenging the use of "Jew/Jews" and advocating either "Judean/Judeans" (to designate a regional connotation) or "Israelite/Israelites" (to designate an ethnic identity). Justification for this is grounded in the modern sense conveyed by "Jew"—a notion of a developed religious identity that would not have been present in the first and second centuries CE but developed after the time of the Mishnah in the fourth century. Others, including some Jewish scholars, have resisted such a retranslation. Until the dust settles on an agreed-upon appropriate translation, it seems best to me to render it as a transliterated form of the Greek word most often used outside of Palestine as a group designator by both insiders and outsiders, hence "*Ioudaios/Ioudaioi*." This seems to me to maintain nicely the very ambiguity of the term. See further John H. Elliott, "Jesus the Israelite Was neither a 'Jew' nor a 'Christian': On Correcting Misleading Nomenclature," *Journal for the Study of the Historical Jesus* 5 (2007): 119–54.

2. David L. Balch, "Paul, Families, and Households," in *Paul in the Greco-Roman World*, ed. J. Paul Sampley (Harrisburg, PA: Trinity Press International, 2003), 258.

3. Andrew Wallace-Hadrill, "*Domus* and *Insulae* in Rome: Families and Housefuls," in *Early Christian Families in Context: An Interdisciplinary Dialogue*, eds. David L. Balch and Carolyn Osiek (Grand Rapids, MI: Eerdmans, 2003), 4; Peter Oakes, *Philippians: From People to Letter*, SNTSMS 110 (Cambridge: Cambridge University Press, 2001), 18; Wayne A. Meeks, *The First Urban Christians: The Social World of the Apostle Paul* (New Haven, CT: Yale University Press, 1983), 30. On the scenario of poor persons living in the houses of their patrons in order to enhance occasions for social networking, see Andrew Wallace-Hadrill, *Houses and Society in Pompeii and Herculaneum* (Princeton, NJ: Princeton University Press, 1994), 45–47.

4. Chaido Koukouli-Chrysantaki, "Colonia Iulia Augusta Philippensis," in *Philippi at the Time of Paul and After His Death*, eds. Charalambos Bakirtzis and Helmut Koester (Harrisburg, PA: Trinity Press International, 1998), 24; Oakes, *Philippians*, 64.

5. Balch, "Paul, Families, and Households," 259.

6. Ibid., 261, with parenthetical page references to Paul Zanker, *Pompeii: Public and Private Life* (Cambridge, MA: Harvard University Press, 1998).

7. Balch, "Paul, Families, and Households," 274, citing *CIL* 4.1136. For a few examples of women as heads of households see G. H. R. Horsley, *New Documents Illustrating Early Christianity 2*: *A Review of the Greek Inscriptions and Papyri Published in 1977*. NewDocs 2 (Macquarie, Australia: The Ancient History Documentary Research Centre, Macquarie University, 1982), 31–32.

8. Balch, "Paul, Families, and Households," 261, with parenthetical page references to Zanker, *Pompeii*. Balch also notes that "Zanker's thesis is based especially on the study of medium and small houses, the size house in which Christians may have lived and worshipped" ("Paul, Families, and Households," 261).

9. See John R. Clarke, *Art in the Lives of Ordinary Romans: Visual Representation and Non-elite Viewers in Italy, 100 B.C.–A.D. 315* (Berkeley and Los Angeles: University of California Press, 2003), 26–31.

10. Susan Treggiari, "Women in the Time of Augustus," in *The Cambridge Companion to the Age of Augustus*, ed. Karl Galinsky (Cambridge: Cambridge University Press, 2005), 134; cf. Meeks, *First Urban Christians*, 30.

11. Bella Vivante, *Daughters of Gaia: Women in the Ancient Mediterranean World*, Praeger Series on the Ancient World (Westport, CT: Praeger, 2007),

54. For the following I am aided by the helpful summary of Jerome H. Neyrey, "Clean/Unclean, Pure/Polluted, and Holy/Profane: The Idea and the System of Purity," in *The Social Sciences and New Testament Interpretation*, ed. Richard L. Rohrbaugh (Peabody, MA: Hendrickson, 1996), 87–91, and by Bruce J. Malina, *The New Testament World: Insights from Cultural Anthropology*, 3rd ed. (Louisville, KY: Westminster John Knox, 2001), 161–97.

12. Sarah B. Pomeroy, *Goddesses, Whores, Wives, and Slaves: Women in Classical Antiquity* (New York: Dorset Press, 1975), 150.

13. Bruce J. Malina and Jerome H. Neyrey, "Honor and Shame in Luke-Acts: Pivotal Values of the Mediterranean World," in *The Social World of Luke-Acts: Models for Interpretation*, ed. Jerome H. Neyrey (Peabody, MA: Hendrickson, 1991), 62.

14. Pomeroy, *Goddesses*, 153, citing Aulus Gellius, *Attic Nights*, 10.23; Plutarch, *Roman Questions 6*, cf. Plutarch, *Moralia*, 265b.

15. Vivante, *Daughters of Gaia*, 51, 57.

16. *Laudatio Turiae* col. 1.30-4; translation in Judith Evans Grubbs, "The Family," in *A Companion to the Roman Empire*, ed. David S. Potter, Blackwell Companions to the Ancient World (Malden, MA: Blackwell, 2006), 314.

17. *CIL* 2.1211; translation in Pomeroy, *Goddesses*, 199.

18. Bruce W. Winter, *Roman Wives, Roman Widows: The Appearance of New Women and the Pauline Communities* (Grand Rapids, MI: Eerdmans, 2003), 18.

19. Vivante, *Daughters of Gaia*, 55.

20. R. A. Bauman, *Women and Politics in Ancient Rome* (London: Routledge, 1992), 105, quoted in Winter, *Roman Wives*, 39. For details of Augustus' legislation and responses to it see Winter, *Roman Wives*, 39–74. Cf. Treggiari "Women in the Time of Augustus," 144–45.

21. For the following I am largely indebted to Pomeroy, *Goddesses*, 150–55, and Peter Garnsey and Richard Saller, *The Roman Empire: Economy, Society and Culture* (London: Duckworth, 1987), 130–36.

22. Horsley, *New Documents 2*, 29–31; Lilian Portefaix, *Sisters Rejoice: Paul's Letter to the Philippians and Luke-Acts as Received by First-Century Philippian Women*, ConBNT 20 (Stockholm: Almquist & Wiksell, 1988), 9 n. 4; Vivante, *Daughters of Gaia*, 59. For papyri examples of how the *ius liberorum* was employed in antiquity, see Horsley, *New Documents 2*, 29–32, although he cautions that what was applicable in Egypt may not have been so in Macedonia in the first century.

23. I have chosen the word "Romanized" rather than "Hellenized" in order to put emphasis on the impact of such things as the Augustan reforms. It is certainly the case that the Romans generally were greatly

influenced by the Greek culture of the peoples that they conquered in the second and first centuries BCE. Nevertheless, there were also certain distinctions to being Roman that they introduced to the Greek cultural contexts. These were not static, however, and thus we will focus on the impact of Augustus on post-Augustan urban life.

24. The writer of the Pastoral Epistles views widows as a financial burden to the Jesus group (1 Tim 5:4, 8, 16), also noting that some widows go from house to house saying things they should not (1 Tim 5:13) while others have broken their pledges to celibacy (1 Tim 5:11-12; probably "virgin-widows" who have later decided to marry). The writer stipulates that young widows receive no aid and should (re)marry while older widows may receive aid but should look first to their families. The Pastor seems to be suggesting that only rich, old widows who were self-sufficient could take part in group leadership, if in fact this is what it means to register widows (1 Tim 5:9; "put on a list"). The writer is moving the Jesus group into a stable phase in which roles are defined through the domestication and silencing of women. He sees marriage as bringing honor and as normative, a cultural view shared by the wider society in which he lives.

25. Bruce J. Malina and John J. Pilch, *Social-Science Commentary on the Book of Acts* (Minneapolis, MN: Fortress, 2008), 214–15.

26. Ibid., 117.

27. Cornelius Nepos (first century BCE), *Lives of Foreign Generals*, praef. 6, cited in Winter, *Roman Wives*, 34. See also Valarius Maximus, *Memorable Doings and Sayings*, 2.1.2; Balch, "Paul, Families, and Households," 274.

28. Balch, "Paul, Families, and Households," 273.

29. On the foodstuffs of the Greco-Roman diet, including numerous recipes, see Ilaria Gozzini Giacosa, *A Taste of Ancient Rome* (Chicago, IL: University of Chicago Press, 1992) and Patrick Faas, *Around the Roman Table: Food and Feasting in Ancient Rome* (Chicago, IL: University of Chicago Press, 1994). For arguments against the view that only the minority elite could afford to eat meat and fish, while the majority poor ate a vegetarian diet, and a rather stark one at that, see Veronika E. Grimm, "On Food and the Body," in *A Companion to the Roman Empire*, ed. David S. Potter, Blackwell Companions to the Ancient World (Malden, MA: Blackwell, 2006), 354–68.

30. See Susan Treggiari, "Lower Class Women in the Roman Economy," *Florilegium* 1 (1979): 71, 78.

31. Oakes, *Philippians*, 64.

32. Ibid. Sterck-Degueldre likewise argues that purple dealership places Lydia in a lucrative (and attractive) profession that would have

led to her being more comfortable than most, albeit not rich (*Eine Frau namens Lydia*, WUNT II/176 [Tübingen: Mohr Siebeck, 2004], 234–38).

33. Oakes, *Philippians*, 59.

34. That Paul addresses some issues of conflict (Phil 2:2-4; 4:2-3) suggests that there are agonistic challenges within the group, pointing to cross-household adherents. That he acknowledges what seems to be a substantial benefaction to him (4:10-19), received on more than one occasion (4:16), would suggest the presence of at least one, perhaps a few, wealthy householders; see further Richard S. Ascough, *Paul's Macedonian Associations: The Social Context of 1 Thessalonians and Philippians*, WUNT II/161 (Tübingen: Mohr Siebeck, 2003), 150–52.

35. For a summary of the debate on Romanization see Roman Roth, *Styling Romanisation: Pottery and Society in Central Italy*, Cambridge Classical Studies (Cambridge: Cambridge University Press, 2007), 9–39.

Notes to Chapter 3 (pages 58–69)

1. The following description of these ranks and their interrelationships is summarized from Peter Garnsey and Richard Saller, *The Roman Empire: Economy, Society and Culture* (London: Duckworth, 1987), 112–25.

2. Masters could turn over the daily operation of their workshops or stores to a slave, giving him freedom to pocket any profits beyond what the master expected. The *peculium* allowed slaves to have money for capital expenses and to own property and other slaves; for details see ibid., 119–20.

3. Bruce J. Malina and John J. Pilch, *Social-Science Commentary on the Letters of Paul* (Minneapolis: Fortress, 2006), 359–62; see also Louise J. Lawrence, *Reading with Anthropology: Exhibiting Aspects of New Testament Religion* (Milton Keynes: Paternoster, 2005), 11.

4. Translation in Sarah B. Pomeroy, *Goddesses, Whores, Wives, and Slaves: Women in Classical Antiquity* (New York: Dorset Press, 1975), 177.

5. In such a world riches constituted social injustice. To be labeled "rich" was not just an economic statement but a social and moral statement. Of course, this is the view from below; for the elite the opposite would be the case (wealth equals high moral character). Thus, the rich ruler (Luke 18:18-25) has more at stake in his confrontation with Jesus than just loss of wealth; his moral character is on the line. In the story, he fails to redeem himself morally, showing the fundamental nature of those who are rich (cf. Zacchaeus). Poverty meant not only that one had been

dealt an injustice somewhere along the way; it also meant that one was powerless to change things. The poor for Luke include the imprisoned, the blind, the debtors, the crippled, the lame, and beggars (Luke 4:18-19; cf. 7:21-23). All these people are without power and thus without recourse to gaining their share of the pie. For those with power, wealth naturally followed. In antiquity the poor were the weak and the rich were the strong.

6. Judith Evans Grubbs, "The Family," in *A Companion to the Roman Empire*, ed. David S. Potter, Blackwell Companions to the Ancient World (Malden, MA: Blackwell, 2006), 313; Pomeroy, *Goddesses*, 185.

7. Cited by Pomeroy, *Goddesses*, 169–70.

8. For the following description of the "new" women in Rome I am particularly indebted to Phyllis Culham, "Did Roman Women Have an Empire?," in *Inventing Ancient Culture: Historicism, Periodization, and the Ancient World*, ed. Mark Golden and Peter Toohey (London: Routledge, 1997), 192–204; Bruce W. Winter, *Roman Wives, Roman Widows: The Appearance of New Women and the Pauline Communities* (Grand Rapids, MI: Eerdmans, 2003), 4–6, 17–31. The first three chapters of Winter's book are worth reading carefully.

9. Pomeroy, *Goddesses*, 189.

10. Winter, *Roman Wives*, 33.

11. See ibid., 32–37; Ramsay MacMullen, "Women in Public in the Roman Empire," *Historia* 29 (1980): 217–18; Culham, "Roman Women," 202–3; Wayne A. Meeks, *The First Urban Christians: The Social World of the Apostle Paul* (New Haven, CT: Yale University Press, 1983), 23.

12. Quoted in Winter, *Roman Wives*, 34; Culham, "Roman Women," 202.

Notes to Chapter 4 (pages 70–81)

1. Epictetus, *Discourses*, 3.13.9, translation in Everett Ferguson, *Backgrounds of Early Christianity* (Grand Rapids, MI: Eerdmans, 1987), 64. On Roman trade and trade routes, see ibid., 62–67. On travel in Roman antiquity, see Wayne A. Meeks, *The First Urban Christians: The Social World of the Apostle Paul* (New Haven, CT: Yale University Press, 1983), 17–18, and more generally Lionel Casson, *Travel in the Ancient World* (Baltimore, MD: Johns Hopkins University Press, 1974), 115–299.

2. Ronald F. Hock, *The Social Context of Paul's Ministry: Tentmaking and Apostleship* (Philadelphia, PA: Fortress, 1980), 35; A second-century CE

writer named Lucian illustrates this well: "Their trades, however, were petty, laborious, and barely able to supply them with just enough" (*The Runways*, 13, LCL).

3. Hock, *Social Context*, 36. Helpful for the following material is Joseph H. Hellerman, *Reconstructing Honor in Roman Philippi: Carmen Christi as Cursus Pudorum*, SNTSMS 132 (Cambridge: Cambridge University Press, 2005), 19–21; cf. Sandra R. Joshel, *Work, Identity, and Legal Status at Rome: A Study of the Occupational Inscriptions* (Norman, OK: University of Oklahoma Press, 1992), 63–69.

4. Quoted in Hellerman, *Reconstructing Honor*, 20–21. Hellerman points out that the descriptive "wretched gallows-bird" literally indicates "one destined for crucifixion," that is, the type of punishment meant to be most shameful and status-degrading.

5. Bella Vivante, *Daughters of Gaia: Women in the Ancient Mediterranean World*, Praeger Series on the Ancient World (Westport, CT: Praeger, 2007), 95.

6. Ibid., 106.

7. Location IX, 7, 1. John R. Clarke, *Art in the Lives of Ordinary Romans: Visual representation and Non-elite Viewers in Italy, 100 B.C.–A.D. 315* (Berkeley and Los Angeles: University of California Press, 2003), 111; cf. John R. Clarke, *Roman Life: 100 B.C. to A.D. 200* (New York: Abrams, 2007), 64; Sarah B. Pomeroy, *Goddesses, Whores, Wives, and Slaves: Women in Classical Antiquity* (New York: Dorset Press, 1975), 200.

8. *CIL* 10.810 and 811. Translation in David L. Balch, "Paul, Families, and Households," in *Paul in the Greco-Roman World*, ed. J. Paul Sampley (Harrisburg, PA: Trinity Press International, 2003), 274. The building measures ca. 60 x 40 meters (location VII.ix.1/67).

9. Susan Treggiari, "Jobs for Women," *American Journal of Ancient History* 1 (1976): 91.

10. On the use of *porphyropōlis* in antiquity see G. H. R. Horsley, *New Documents Illustrating Early Christianity 2: A Review of the Greek Inscriptions and Papyri Published in 1977*, NewDocs 2 (Macquarie, Australia: The Ancient History Documentary Research Centre, Macquarie University, 1982), 26–27, who notes a number of inscriptions, including some that mention women.

11. Colin J. Hemer, *The Letters to the Seven Churches of Asia in Their Local Setting*, JSNTSup 11 (Sheffield: Sheffield Academic Press, 1986), 54.

12. *Histories*, 6.53; translation in Hellerman, *Reconstructing Honor*, 16.

13. *Life of Lucullus*, 39.50–61.2; translation in Naphtali Lewis and Meyer Reinhold, eds., *Roman Civilization: Selected Readings*, vol. 1, *The Republic*

and the Augustan Age, 3rd ed. (New York: Columbia University Press, 1990), 493.

14. For the Greek text see Peter Pilhofer, *Philippi*, Band II, *Katalog der Inschriften von Philippi*, WUNT 119 (Tübingen: Mohr Siebeck, 2000), no. 697. The inscription was found on a slab of white marble by Stauros Mertzides in 1872 in a military post that he claims was subsequently destroyed. The trustworthiness of this inscription has been questioned by some scholars of epigraphy but affirmed by others, including Peter Pilhofer, *Philippi*, Band I, *Die erste christliche Gemeinde Europas*, WUNT 87 (Tübingen: Mohr Siebeck, 1995), 180–82. On the importance of purple dyeing at Thyatira, see T. R. S. Broughton, "Roman Asia," in *An Economic Survey of Ancient Rome*, ed. Tenny Frank, vol. 4 (Baltimore, MD: Johns Hopkins University Press, 1938), 819. David Magie notes that the guild of purple dyers in Thyatira was "evidently unusually prosperous," citing a number of inscriptions, including *CIG* 3496, 3497, and 3498 (*Roman Rule in Asia Minor* [Princeton, NJ: Princeton University Press, 1950], 48).

15. Ivoni Richter Reimer, *Women in the Acts of the Apostles: A Feminist Liberation Perspective* (Minneapolis, MN: Fortress, 1995), 105, citing *CIG* 2519. Reimer cites further evidence from *CIL* 1.1413; 2.2235; 5.1044; 6.984, 4016, 9848, 32454; 14.473, 2433.

16. For details see Richard S. Ascough, *Paul's Macedonian Associations: The Social Context of 1 Thessalonians and Philippians*, WUNT II/161 (Tübingen: Mohr Siebeck, 2003), 54–59.

17. Pilhofer, *Philippi* II, no. 340. Another inscription is dedicated to the same three deities, Liber, Libera, and Hercules, and was set up by a woman named Pomponia Hilara (Pilhofer, *Philippi* II, no. 339); it may therefore attest to the same group as in no. 340.

Notes to Chapter 5 (pages 82–95)

1. I do not agree with Reimer (*Women in the Acts of the Apostles: A Feminist Liberation Perspective* [Minneapolis, MN: Fortress, 1995], 96) that appellations such as God (*theos*), God Almighty (*theos hypsistos*), or Lord (*kyrios*) were regarded by non-*Ioudaioi* as designations for the God of Israel; for evidence see Richard S. Ascough, *Paul's Macedonian Associations: The Social Context of 1 Thessalonians and Philippians*, WUNT II/161 (Tübingen: Mohr Siebeck, 2003), 195–201. [Editor's note: Monotheism means the belief in the existence and worship of one and only one God (Greek: *monos* means only [one]); henotheism means the belief in and worship of one God at the

expense of and in face of the existence of many other Gods (Greek: *hen* means one [of many]). Israel's profession of faith presumes the existence of many gods, with their God being number one ("Hear, O Israel: The Lᴏʀᴅ is *our* God, the Lᴏʀᴅ alone" [Deut 6:4; emphasis added]). Exod 20:3 "[Y]ou shall have no other gods before me" in the Ten Commandments requires giving precedence in all things to the God of Israel. As Paul states in 1 Cor 8:5-6: "Indeed, even though there may be so-called gods in heaven or on earth—as in fact there are many gods and many lords—yet for us there is one God, the Father, from whom are all things and for whom we exist, and one Lord, Jesus Christ, through whom are all things and through whom we exist." These statements presume henotheism.]

2. See, for example, A. Thomas Kraabel, "The Disappearance of the 'God-fearers,'" *Numen* 28 (1981): 113–26. I trace this debate up to the mid-90s in *What Are They Saying About the Formation of Pauline Churches?* (New York: Paulist Press, 1998), 14–20.

3. Lee I. Levine, *The Ancient Synagogue: The First Thousand Years*, 2nd ed. (New Haven, CT: Yale University Press, 2005), 118–20. She may have held the office by virtue of being the wife of the high priest (so Ramsay MacMullen, "Women in Public in the Roman Empire," *Historia* 29 [1980]: 213–14), but would nevertheless have been expected to participate in the rituals of the imperial cult. In attempting to establish how much, if any, Jewish adherence is implied in Luke's use of phrases such as "fearer/ worshiper of God" it is important to recognize that there is little to be gained by touting the once ubiquitous but now largely discounted notion of first-century "Judaism" or even "Diaspora Judaism." Such generalizations of monolithic concepts have proven to be myopic, although they have endured in some scholarly discourse.

4. Levine, *Ancient Synagogue*, 100–102 and 97 n. 98.

5. That interest in or even adherence to things Judean immediately led to Israelite henotheism or monotheism is an unjustified assumption among New Testament scholars. Even in communities founded by Paul and grounded in Israelite henotheism, there continued to be interest and practice in polytheistic traditions and customs, as demonstrated by letters written by Paul or in his name to provide a corrective (1 Cor 10:14-22 and 11:28-30; Col 2:8-23; Eph 4:17–5:20, perhaps Gal 4:3, 8-10).

6. On the discussion of the exact location of the *proseuchē* see Wayne A. Meeks, *The First Urban Christians: The Social World of the Apostle Paul* (New Haven, CT: Yale University Press, 1983), 211 n. 237. There existed a stream on both the east side and the west side of the ancient city of Philippi. Additionally, a larger river, the Gangites, lay just over two kilometers from the city center, close to a commemorative arch that marks

the western edge of the sacred boundary of the city. Meeks is surely correct in his assertion that the lack of any concrete evidence makes all speculation about the *proseuchē*'s exact location of doubtful value. The significance of its proximity to water, on the other hand, may be of some interest, as we shall discuss below.

7. Reimer, *Women*, 74, 77.

8. For arguments for a building see Martin Hengel, "Proseuche und Synagoge: Jüdische Gemeinde, Gotteshaus und Gottesdienst in der Diaspora und in Palästina," in *Tradition und Glaube: Das frühe Christentum in seiner Umwelt*, G. Jeremias, et al., eds. (Göttingen: Vandenhoech & Ruprecht, 1971), 171. On an outdoor location, see C. K. Barrett, *The Acts of the Apostles*, vol. 2, ICC (London and New York: T & T Clark, 1998), 781–82.

9. Bruce J. Malina and John J. Pilch, *Social-Science Commentary on the Book of Acts* (Minneapolis, MN: Fortress, 2008), 117; cf. Bruce J. Malina, *Timothy: Paul's Closest Associate*, Paul's Social Network: Brothers and Sisters in Faith (Collegeville, MN: Liturgical Press, 2008), 106.

10. This requirement appears in later rabbinic sources such as *b. Berakhot* 6a, from the second century CE—"Whenever God comes to a synagogue and does not find ten men for prayer, he immediately becomes angry" (translation in Levine, *Ancient Synagogue*, 446 n. 198; cf. 200); see also in Levine's book *y. Berakhot* 5, 1, 8d-9a (p. 200); *m. Megillah* 4.3 (p. 555); *y. Megillah* 4, 4, 75a (p. 556); *b. Megillah* 23b (p. 565 n. 155); *Tractate Soferim* 10, 6 (p. 555 n. 107; p. 590 n. 300). That this requirement may go back to the first century is suggested by Josephus, *Jewish War*, 2.146 and the Qumran document *1QS* 6.3; 6.7. That women could participate in synagogue services, and perhaps even form *part* of the *minyan* is possible (see *b. Megillah* 23a and the discussion in Bernadette J. Brooten, *Women Leaders in the Ancient Synagogue*, Brown Judaic Studies 36 [Atlanta: Scholars Press, 1982], 94–95), but a synagogue of women is nowhere attested. To date, no evidence of a first-century synagogue or a large Jewish population at Philippi, or more widely in Macedonia, has been found (see Ascough, *Paul's Macedonian Associations*, 191–212, esp. 201–5). There did exist in Thyatira a Jewish community that may explain Lydia's contact with Judaism, although we do not know when she left that city, or what other of the many deities at Thyatira she may have encountered, deities such as Asclepius, Dionysus, Artemis, and Isis, the latter who is even called "Lydia" on an inscription (*SIRIS* 371).

11. Reimer, *Women*, 107, citing Pliny the Elder, *Natural History*, 19.47.

12. Valerie Ann Abrahamsen, *Women and Worship at Philippi: Diana/Artemis and Other Cults in the Early Christian Era* (Portland, OR: Astarte Shell Press, 1995), 25–67.

13. Lilian Portefaix, *Sisters Rejoice: Paul's Letter to the Philippians and Luke-Acts as Received by First-Century Philippian Women*, ConBNT 20 (Stockholm: Almquist & Wiksell, 1988), 101.

14. Chaido Koukouli-Chrysantaki, "Colonia Iulia Augusta Philippensis," in *Philippi at the Time of Paul and After His Death*, eds. Charalambos Bakirtzis and Helmut Koester (Harrisburg, PA: Trinity Press International, 1998), 25.

15. Amy Richlin, "Carrying Water in a Sieve: Class and the Body in Roman Women's Religion," in *Women and Goddess Traditions: In Antiquity and Today*, ed. Karen L. King (Minneapolis, MN: Fortress, 1997), 336.

16. Sharon Kelly Heyob, *The Cult of Isis Among Women in the Graeco-Roman World*, EPRO 51 (Leiden: Brill, 1975), 20, 110; Dio Cassius, *Roman History*, 49.40.3; Plutarch, *Parallel Lives*, "Antony," 50. The cult was popular throughout Macedonia. The sanctuary to the Egyptian gods at Philippi was built on the side of the acropolis hill, sometime during the imperial period, although a precise date is hard to establish. Koukouli-Chrysantaki argues that the sanctuary of the Egyptian gods, along with the rock sanctuaries on the acropolis, date to the second century CE, but notes that cult centers may have existed on those same sites during the first century ("Colonia," 18).

17. It was only later, in the second and third generation of Jesus believers, that female leadership roles became more restricted and men assumed almost complete control in the proto-orthodox churches. We see the process developing in the Deutero-Pauline and Pastoral Letters. These developments are part of a wider response to "new" women in the Roman Empire as the first century was drawing to a close. After the liberties gained through the Augustan reforms, the windows of opportunity began disappearing with the suppression of women's freedoms.

Notes to Conclusion (pages 96–100)

1. Valerie Ann Abrahamsen, "Women at Philippi: The Pagan and Christian Evidence," *Journal of Feminist Studies in Religion* 3, no. 2 (1987): 19.

2. For details see ibid., 23–29.

BIBLIOGRAPHY

Abrahamsen, Valerie Ann. "Women at Philippi: The Pagan and Christian Evidence." *Journal of Feminist Studies in Religion* 3, no. 2 (1987): 17–30.

———. *Women and Worship at Philippi: Diana/Artemis and Other Cults in the Early Christian Era.* Portland, OR: Astarte Shell Press, 1995.

Ascough, Richard S. "Civic Pride at Philippi: The Text-Critical Problem of Acts 16:12." *NTS* 44 (1996): 93–103.

———. *Paul's Macedonian Associations: The Social Context of 1 Thessalonians and Philippians.* WUNT II/161. Tübingen: Mohr Siebeck, 2003.

———. *What Are They Saying About the Formation of Pauline Churches?* New York and Mahwah: Paulist Press, 1998.

Balch, David L. "Paul, Families, and Households." In *Paul in the Greco-Roman World,* edited by J. Paul Sampley, 258–92. Harrisburg, PA: Trinity Press International, 2003.

Barrett, C. K. *The Acts of the Apostles.* ICC. London and New York: T & T Clark, 1998.

Bauman, R. A. *Women and Politics in Ancient Rome.* London: Routledge, 1992.

Brooten, Bernadette J. *Women Leaders in the Ancient Synagogue.* Brown Judaic Studies 36. Atlanta, GA: Scholars Press, 1982.

Broughton, T. R. S. "Roman Asia." In *An Economic Survey of Ancient Rome,* vol. 4. Edited by Tenny Frank, 499–916. Baltimore: Johns Hopkins University Press, 1938.

Casson, Lionel. *Travel in the Ancient World.* Baltimore, MD: Johns Hopkins University Press, 1994.

Clarke, John R. *Art in the Lives of Ordinary Romans: Visual Representation and Non-elite Viewers in Italy, 100 B.C.–A.D. 315.* Berkeley and Los Angeles: University of California Press, 2003.

———. *Roman Life: 100 B.C. to A.D. 200.* New York: Abrams, 2007.

Collart, Paul. *Philippes, ville de Macédonia, depuis ses origines jusqu'à la fin de la l'époque romaine*. Thèse. Université de Genève 85. Paris: Boccard, 1937.

Cross, F. L., and E. A. Livingstone, eds. *The Oxford Dictionary of the Christian Church*. 3rd ed. Oxford: Oxford University Press, 1997.

Culham, Phyllis. "Did Roman Women Have an Empire?" In *Inventing Ancient Culture: Historicism, Periodization, and the Ancient World*, edited by Mark Golden and Peter Toohey, 192–204. London: Routledge, 1997.

Elliott, John H. "Jesus the Israelite Was neither a 'Jew' nor a 'Christian': On Correcting Misleading Nomenclature." *Journal for the Study of the Historical Jesus* 5 (2007): 119–54.

Faas, Patrick. *Around the Roman Table: Food and Feasting in Ancient Rome*. Chicago, IL: University of Chicago Press, 1994.

Ferguson, Everett. *Backgrounds of Early Christianity*. Grand Rapids, MI: Eerdmans, 1987.

Garnsey, Peter, and Richard Saller. *The Roman Empire: Economy, Society and Culture*. London: Duckworth, 1987.

Giacosa, Ilaria Gozzini. *A Taste of Ancient Rome*. Chicago, IL: University of Chicago Press, 1992.

Grimm, Veronika E. "On Food and the Body." In *A Companion to the Roman Empire*, edited by David S. Potter, 354–68. Blackwell Companions to the Ancient World. Malden, MA: Blackwell, 2006.

Grubbs, Judith Evans. "The Family." In *A Companion to the Roman Empire*, edited by David S. Potter, 312–26. Blackwell Companions to the Ancient World. Malden, MA: Blackwell, 2006.

Hellerman, Joseph H. *Reconstructing Honor in Roman Philippi: Carmen Christi as* Cursus Pudorum. SNTSMS 132. Cambridge: Cambridge University Press, 2005.

Hemer, Colin J. *The Letters to the Seven Churches of Asia in Their Local Setting*. JSNTSup 11. Sheffield: Sheffield Academic Press, 1986.

———. "The Cities of Revelation." In *New Documents Illustrating Early Christianity 3*, edited by G. H. R. Horsley, 51–58. NewDocs 3. Macquarie, Australia: The Ancient History Documentary Research Centre, Macquarie University, 1983.

Hengel, Martin. "Proseuche und Synagoge: Jüdische Gemeinde, Gotteshaus und Gottesdienst in der Diaspora und in Palästina." In *Tradition und Glaube: Das frühe Christentum in seiner Umwelt*, edited by G. Jeremias, et al., 157–84. Göttingen: Vandenhoech & Ruprecht, 1971.

Heyob, Sharon Kelly. *The Cult of Isis Among Women in the Graeco-Roman World*. EPRO 51. Leiden: Brill, 1975.

Hock, Ronald F. *The Social Context of Paul's Ministry: Tentmaking and Apostleship*. Philadelphia, PA: Fortress, 1980.

Hofstede, Geert. "Foreword." In *Individualism and Collectivism: Theory, Method, and Applications,* edited by U. Kim, H. C. Triandis, C. Kagitcibasi, S.-C. Choi, and G. Yoon, ix–xiv. Thousand Oaks, CA: Sage, 1994.

Horsley, G. H. R. *New Documents Illustrating Early Christianity 2: A Review of the Greek Inscriptions and Papyri Published in 1977*. NewDocs 2. Macquarie, Australia: The Ancient History Documentary Research Centre, Macquarie University, 1982.

Joshel, Sandra R. *Work, Identity, and Legal Status at Rome: A Study of the Occupational Inscriptions*. Norman, OK: University of Oklahoma Press, 1992.

Koukouli-Chrysantaki, Chaido. "Colonia Iulia Augusta Philippensis." In *Philippi at the Time of Paul and After His Death*, edited by Charalambos Bakirtzis and Helmut Koester, 5–35. Harrisburg, PA: Trinity Press International, 1998.

Kraabel, A. Thomas. "The Disappearance of the 'God-fearers.'" *Numen* 28 (1981): 113–26.

Lawrence, Louise J. *Reading with Anthropology: Exhibiting Aspects of New Testament Religion*. Milton Keynes: Paternoster, 2005.

Levine, Lee I. *The Ancient Synagogue: The First Thousand Years*. 2nd ed. New Haven, CT: Yale University Press, 2005.

Lewis, Naphtali, and Meyer Reinhold, eds. *Roman Civilization: Selected Readings*. Vol. 1, *The Republic and the Augustan Age*. 3rd ed. New York: Columbia University Press, 1990.

Lüdemann, Gerd. *Early Christianity According to the Traditions in Acts: A Commentary*. Minneapolis, MN: Fortress, 1989.

MacMullen, Ramsay. "Women in Public in the Roman Empire." *Historia* 29 (1980): 208–18.

Magie, David. *Roman Rule in Asia Minor*. Princeton, NJ: Princeton University Press, 1950.

Malina, Bruce J. "Understanding New Testament Persons." In *The Social Sciences and New Testament Interpretation*, edited by Richard L. Rohrbaugh, 41–61. Peabody, PA: Hendrickson, 1996.

———. *The New Testament World: Insights from Cultural Anthropology*. 3rd ed. Louisville, KY: Westminster John Knox, 2001.

————. *Timothy: Paul's Closest Associate*. Paul's Social Network: Brothers and Sisters in Faith. Collegeville, MN: Liturgical Press, 2008.

Malina, Bruce J., and Jerome H. Neyrey. "Honor and Shame in Luke-Acts: Pivotal Values of the Mediterranean World." In *The Social World of Luke-Acts: Models for Interpretation*, edited by Jerome H. Neyrey, 25–65. Peabody, PA: Hendrickson, 1991.

Malina, Bruce J., and John J. Pilch. *Social-Science Commentary on the Letters of Paul*. Minneapolis, MN: Fortress, 2006.

————. *Social-Science Commentary on the Book of Acts*. Minneapolis, MN: Fortress, 2008.

Meeks, Wayne A. *The First Urban Christians: The Social World of the Apostle Paul*. New Haven, CT: Yale University Press, 1983.

Neyrey, Jerome H. "Clean/Unclean, Pure/Polluted, and Holy/Profane: The Idea and the System of Purity." In *The Social Sciences and New Testament Interpretation*, edited by Richard L. Rohrbaugh, 80–104. Peabody, MA: Hendrickson, 1996.

Oakes, Peter. *Philippians: From People to Letter*. SNTSMS 110. Cambridge: Cambridge University Press, 2001.

Papazoglou, Fanoula. "Macedonia Under the Romans." In *Macedonia: 4000 Years of Greek History and Civilization*, edited by M. B. Sakellariou, 192–207. Athens: Ekdotike Athenon S.A., 1983.

Pilch, John J. *Stephen: Paul and the Hellenist Israelites*. Paul's Social Network: Brothers and Sisters in Faith. Collegeville, MN: Liturgical Press, 2008.

Pilhofer, Peter. *Philippi*. Band I. *Die erste christliche Gemeinde Europas*. WUNT 87. Tübingen: Mohr Siebeck, 1995.

————. *Philippi*. Band II. *Katalog der Inschriften von Philippi*. WUNT 119. Tübingen: Mohr Siebeck, 2000.

Pomeroy, Sarah B. *Goddesses, Whores, Wives, and Slaves: Women in Classical Antiquity*. New York: Schocken Books, 1975.

Portefaix, Lilian. *Sisters Rejoice: Paul's Letter to the Philippians and Luke-Acts as Received by First-Century Philippian Women*. ConBNT 20. Stockholm: Almquist & Wiksell, 1988.

Ramsay, W. M. *The Letters to the Seven Churches*. Edited by Mark W. Wilson. Updated ed. Peabody, MA: Hendrickson, 1994.

Reimer, Ivoni Richter. *Women in the Acts of the Apostles: A Feminist Liberation Perspective*. Minneapolis, MN: Fortress, 1995.

Richlin, Amy. "Carrying Water in a Sieve: Class and the Body in Roman Women's Religion." In *Women and Goddess Traditions: In Antiquity and Today*, edited by Karen L. King, 330–74. Minneapolis, MN: Fortress, 1997.

Rohrbaugh, Richard L. "The Preindustrial City." In *The Social Sciences and New Testament Interpretation*, edited by Richard L. Rohrbaugh, 107–25. Peabody, MA: Hendrickson, 1996.

Roth, Roman. *Styling Romanisation: Pottery and Society in Central Italy*. Cambridge Classical Studies. Cambridge: Cambridge University Press, 2007.

Sterck-Degueldre, Jean-Pierre. *Eine Frau namens Lydia*. WUNT II/176. Tübingen: Mohr Siebeck, 2004.

Touratsoglou, Ioannis. *Macedonia: History, Monuments, Museums*. Athens: Ekdotike Athenon, 1995.

Triandis, H. C. *Individualism and Collectivism*. Boulder, CO: Westview Press, 1995.

Treggiari, Susan. "Jobs for Women." *American Journal of Ancient History* 1 (1976): 76–104.

———. "Lower Class Women in the Roman Economy." *Florilegium* 1 (1979): 65–86.

———. "Women in the Time of Augustus." In *The Cambridge Companion to the Age of Augustus*, edited by Karl Galinsky, 130–47. Cambridge: Cambridge University Press, 2005.

Vivante, Bella. *Daughters of Gaia: Women in the Ancient Mediterranean World*. Praeger Series on the Ancient World. Westport, CT: Praeger, 2007.

Wallace-Hadrill, Andrew. *Houses and Society in Pompeii and Herculaneum*. Princeton, NJ: Princeton University Press, 1994.

———. "*Domus* and *Insulae* in Rome: Families and Housefuls." In *Early Christian Families in Context: An Interdisciplinary Dialogue*, edited by David L. Balch and Carolyn Osiek, 3–18. Grand Rapids, MI: Eerdmans, 2003.

Winter, Bruce W. *Roman Wives, Roman Widows: The Appearance of New Women and the Pauline Communities*. Grand Rapids, MI: Eerdmans, 2003.

Witherington III, Ben. *The Acts of the Apostles: A Socio-Rhetorical Commentary*. Grand Rapids, MI: Eerdmans, 1998.

Wortham, Robert A. "The Problem of Anti-Judaism in 1 Thess 2:14-16 and Related Pauline Texts." *BTB* 25 (1995): 37–44.

Zanker, Paul. *Pompeii: Public and Private Life*. Cambridge, MA: Harvard University Press, 1998.

INDEX OF GRECO-ROMAN DOCUMENTS

Ancient Writings and Inscriptions

INDEX
OF PERSONS AND SUBJECTS